Y0-BBY-382

KICKSTART TO
SEEING YOURSELF | CAITLIN
THE WAY GOD DOES | ZICK

"My friend, you are holding a book that wasn't just thrown together but a book that shows how Cait climbed out of her own pits of pain. She leaned in, did the work and now has a pathway to freedom she's showing all of us. It's not just ink on these pages, it's her tears, prayers, hopes, dreams, determination and daily choices to go after liberation. If you trust her and the pathway God has given her, I promise your life will be changed. I'm so grateful Cait has written a book our daughters, granddaughters and our own lives can benefit from for years to come."
- **Havilah Cunnington,** Founder of Truth to Table and Author of *Stronger Than the Struggle*

"Caitlin is the real deal! Sharing so realistically about her own story that it will bring light to every hidden corner of yours. But she doesn't leave you there, she shows us that love, forgiveness & change are possible even in today's culture."
- **Rebecca Bender,** CEO & Author, Thought Leader

"In a world surrounding girls with social pressure and a gospel of negative self-image, Caitlin comes in as a force of truth, authenticity, and empowerment. I've not met many women who can confidently celebrate the success of other women without falling into jealousy and envy the way God has graced Caitlin to do so. She carries herself as a true sister, daughter, and mother being an advocate for the message of Jesus to be grasped by girls everywhere which is, "You are loved." I am so excited for this book to be released in this generation of powerful females who need to hear more than ever how truly amazing they are."
- **Becky Johnson,** Youth Pastor, Jesus Culture

"Caitlin addresses more than just the things we do or say; she speaks to the motivations of our hearts. She boldly talks about insecurities, fears, and lies, countering them with God's truth in a way the average woman can understand.

This book would be a great gift for a new believer and those needing encouragement to go deeper with God."
- **Phylicia Masonheimer,** Founder of Driven Women and Author of *Christian Cosmo*

"There are very few women in this generation who can articulate the women's heart like Caitlin Zick. Packed with brilliance and insight, humor too, you can be sure to experience shifts in perspectives as well as being the owner of a whole new crate of hope. What she writes will come from experience, scriptural backup, and revelation that makes me grateful for women who pursue original thought in a personal relationship with our Lord."
- **Carrie Lloyd,** Pastor, Life Coach and Author of *Prude* and *The Virgin Monologues*

"Just when I thought I had seen and heard everything there was on growing in my walk with the Lord. Cait pens this very personal and vulnerable girls chat for the everyday woman. I could find myself on the pages and transforming by the truth she gave. Buckle your seatbelt for an adventure in discovering yourself all over again!"
- **Melinda Watts,** Founder of GLAM Camp for Girls & Recording Artist

"Caitlin has stood by many as they've faced doubt and has screamed truth to the point they walked away believing they could do more than they thought they could. Out of this she has created a real and relatable tool that will help anyone looking at the lies of perfectionism and settling for less right in the face and point them towards the truth that lies between them. If you are struggling with your worth and embracing who you are this book is a power-house resource that you can refer back to since we are all work in progress and need reminders and practice to renew our minds."
- **Michelle Raby,** Pastor and Author of *To Be Known*

Look at You, Girl: Kickstart to Seeing Yourself
the Way God Does
Copyright © 2019 Caitlin Zick

All rights reserved. You may use brief
quotations from this resource in
presentations, articles and books. For all other
uses, please contact for permission at
turnuptruth.com. This book may not be copied
or reprinted for commercial gain or profit.

All Scripture quotations marked (MSG) are
taken from the Holy Bible THE MESSAGE,
copyright © 1993, 1994, 1995, 1996, 2000, 2001,
2002 by Eugene H. Peterson. All Scripture
quotations marked (NIV) are taken from the
Holy Bible New International Version,
copyright © 1973, 1978, 1984. All Scripture
quotations marked (NKJV) are taken from the
Holy Bible New King James Version, copyright
© 1982. All Scripture quotations marked (NLT)
are taken from the Holy Bible New Living
Translation, copyright © 1996, 2004.

Edited by Carina Willeke, Katie Daugherty,
Carrie Huddleston and Cassandra Soars

Cover Design by Ruth Weatherford

glisten & grace

Interior Design by Melissa Jones
www.glistenandgrace.com

ISBN-13: 978-0-578-44359-1

TABLE OF CONTENTS

ACKNOWLEDGEMENTS

To my husband, Cole, for believing in me incessantly; for providing me with space to make this happen. It is no joke with four children and two jobs to make room for writing, but you did it with a joyful heart and always encouraged me to keep going.

To my friend, Havilah, for inviting and pushing me to write. After making many excuses over the years, I'm now being obedient to a prophetic word from five years earlier. Thank you for seeing me the way He does and inviting me to partner with you.

To the girls: the names would be endless here. Girlfriends in my life who've had a front row seat and huge part in influencing so much of what is written on these pages. To the girls I've had the opportunity to love and lead through the years. The girls who met with me over coffee and read over these words, who danced and celebrated with me, who dreamed with me just what might happen in the worlds of girls everywhere when they open this book.

FOREWORD

I can't put my finger on when I met Caitlin, but I can definitely remember the moment I fell in love with her heart. I'd taken a job as the director of Moral Revolution, a ministry focused on cultivating healthy sexuality. We were hosting an event and invited her and her husband to come and speak. They quickly accepted, which was amazing given the fact that they had four young kids and a five-hour round trip drive. But they willingly volunteered and spoke to a room full of forty young leaders.

Sitting in the front row, we listened as they began to unpack their story of marriage, sexuality, and identity. The atmosphere was charged with raw transparency. They took turns sharing their messy, unedited and humorous journey to freedom. I leaned forward in my seat. I could feel it in the room. I could see it on her life.

Caitlin carries a tangible and practical anointing for freedom. Don't let her beauty and joyfulness fool you. She's a straight up warrior. She's been busy for the last decade unpacking her heart and learning tools to get free and then give them away.

As they drove away I said to my husband, "Ben, wouldn't it be amazing if Cole and Cait could be on staff at Moral Revolution? Like, if we had a ton of money? I mean, they are perfect. Gosh, honestly, they could be the directors one day." I knew this was a little odd for me to say. First, because they already had a great job in Sacramento but secondly, it would mean we would be out of a job. It was ridiculous.

Eight months later in a surprising twist of events, we transitioned out of MR, and they packed up their whole lives, kids, dreams and drove to Redding to be the Moral Revolution Directors.

One year later, I sat having coffee with Cait. She shared her heart for women, freedom and her passion to point them to divine identity. I shot back, "Cait, you have to write a book on this!" It was like a match was lit in the room that day and we became engulfed with this passion project.

So, my friend, you are holding a book that wasn't just thrown together but a book that shows how Cait climbed out of her own pits of pain. She leaned in, did the work and now has a pathway to freedom she's showing all of us. It's not just ink on these pages, it's her tears, prayers, hopes, dreams, determination and daily choices to go after liberation. If you trust her and the pathway God has given her, I promise your life will be changed. I'm so grateful Cait has written a book our daughters, granddaughters and our own lives can benefit from for years to come.

- **Havilah Cunnington,**
Founder of Truth to Table
and Author of *Stronger Than the Struggle*

INTRODUCTION

HEY GIRL, HEY I would rather be sitting across the table from you with lattes in hand saying, "Look at you, girl" and talking about the truth of who your Daddy says you are. But I realize I'm limited by time and space, so I'm writing it down to get it in your hands ASAP. My dream is that you would go grab one of your girls and do this with her. I believe from the bottom of my heart that we truly are better together. We are capable of dismantling the insecurities in each other's lives when we do it side-by-side. So grab a girlfriend and some coffee (or tea, or chocolate or Chipotle—whatever fits your fancy) and take a week to kickstart looking at yourselves the way God does.

PSSST..... I also have a confession. I must confess I can never finish a book, even the ones I love the most, that I recommend to everyone I meet, and the books I can't stop talking about. When it really comes down to it, I usually haven't read them from start to finish. Either I've read the first few chapters and been distracted with something else bright and shiny (follow-through is not my strong suit), or I look at the table of contents, find the chapters I think apply most to me and only read those. Unless it's a short and easy read, I probably haven't read it through and through. Eek, I know! All the real book lovers are just crawling in their skin right now. I'm sorry, I'm sorry.

So when creating this book I wanted to keep it simple. Give yourself one week, thirty minutes a day, and pow! You've read a book! Go, girl!

This is a one-week journey to seeing yourself the way God does a little more clearly. I hope you'll gain fresh perspective, get rid of the lies that don't belong in your beautiful mind and walk away in your new pair of shoes—shoes of peace.

GRAB YOUR GIRL

(write name here)

"WE" WEEK
The week WE will do this kickstart!

(write dates here)

"Make a careful exploration of who you are and the work you have been given, and then sink yourself into that. Don't be impressed with yourself. Don't compare yourself with others. Each of you must take responsibility for doing the creative best you can with your own life."
- Galatians 6:4-5 MSG

CHAPTER 1

motivation

CHAPTER ONE

Let's explore who we are and the work we've been given to do. These are two of life's greatest questions: Who am I? What am I here for? To be able to answer these questions without leaning into pride or comparison is so important. Let's take responsibility for the gift of life we've been given and let's be creative and give it our best.

There are so many voices screaming at us about who to be, what to wear, why to change, when to do what. Let's call these voices the "shoulds". They tell us who we "should" be based on the screaming opinions of so many voices coming at us from every angle. Let's remind you of who you were before the world told you who to be.

I love the time before dawn when I can be who I am and not who everyone else tells me I'm supposed to be. No pressure, no performing, no pretense — just simply me. That may sound scary to some of us because our identity is so wrapped up in what people think or say about us. These things are often spoken over us from a young age. Things like: "You're the shy girl, the loud and crazy one, the bossy girl, the girl who always has a boyfriend." Or maybe your identity is wrapped up in what you do—your role in life, your work, your sport, your art, etc. Maybe you're the brain, the athlete, the social media savant, the workaholic, the mom, the list goes on. But who are you when everything else is stripped away?

No titles, no platforms, no cliques, no roles to hide behind—just you.

The problem is that we don't usually look at ourselves through the lens of what God says about us. Instead, we trade the truth for the most recent opinion of someone else. Maybe we don't know the truth because we haven't been told — or maybe we have. We've been told the truth a time or two but the lies that scream at us on the daily have won over. You're not enough. You're too much. You're not like her. You're less than. You're broken. You're a fraud. Who do you think you are?

Let's talk social media. It can be used for so much good and at the same time we judge ourselves based on the number of followers we have on our Instagram or Twitter feeds, which are just a highlight reel. We need to be aware that the number of followers we have on a social media platform has created a value system that is simply not real. You are no more or less valuable if you have 232 followers or 232K followers. We often see ourselves through the opinions of others — parents, friends, loved ones, even people we don't know. And even worse, we see ourselves through our failures and screw-ups. Studies have shown that we receive critiques and negative statements faster than we receive a compliment and that critiques have a more profound effect on us than compliments. As a matter of fact, we need five positive comments for every negative one.

Our life's purpose is far greater than how we will fit into that dress or what we look like in a bikini. We invest so much in our outside, the external, what we look like. Can you imagine if we started out by investing in our souls? I don't need another hair tutorial, I need a good ol' soul tutorial. I don't need someone else to show me how to contour my face with twenty-two different products that each cost $29.95. I need to know how to grow the beauty that doesn't fade. I want to be comfortable in my skin rather than living in a constant state of insecurity about my natural beauty. Can someone please tell me that my value adds up to more than the latest fashion trends, because they're impossible to keep up with? Keeping up, that's the problem. (Sidenote, sister: Did you know that those who work in the fashion industry literally have the goal of making sure the trends are constantly changing?! We don't need to fall victim to this predator. Not to mention if you think about style, it's so that we can stand out when typically we're really all just subconsciously trying to fit in.) I want to get out of this rat race of proving and striving. I want to rest in who He designed me to be. I want to be confident and grounded from the inside. I want to be unmovable.

Well, sister, that's what we are here to do. To set out on a one-week journey to look inside and find out who we are created to be. Today is a day to uncover the filter of nasty lies that we've seen ourselves through for too long. A day to find out what the Word of Life really has to say about us and set that as our unshakeable foundation. A day to let our gratitude turn what we have into enough, more than enough really. When we get thankful, there's no room for bitterness and discontentment. A day to discover the kind of community we want to be a part of and the kind of friend we want to be: one that calls others higher rather than pulling them down. A day to build up our souls, to look at our thoughts, our attitudes and choices and realize we are powerful in them. Lastly, a day to rest— to look at who He made us to be and call it good. To find the peace that is beyond our circumstances, that comes from the Prince of Peace Himself. Even when our life is storming, the boat seems to be sinking and the wind is raging around us, He brings a calmness that kills anxiety. I like to call it "peace that doesn't make sense". That's when you know it's from heaven.

We are living in a time when our identity is under attack more than ever before. We cannot let the enemy continue to take advantage of us. We are not unaware of his schemes (2 Corinthians 2:11). He knows that when we know who we are, when we walk in the fullness of our identity in Christ— as sons and daughters of the King— he loses. We are not victims, we are the victors. When the believers are silent, when they're not speaking life and truth and not living by design— the enemy comes in with a counterfeit and confusion. He's confusing our generation's sexual identities by making people believe that there are more than two options. When we take it back, all the way back to Genesis— it's super clear, "He created them male and female, and he blessed them and called them 'human'." (Genesis 5:2) He continues to twist the meaning of masculinity and femininity. We also take it back and remember he's been subtle and skilled in deceit from the beginning.

"Now the serpent was more crafty than any of the wild animals the Lord God had made. He said to the woman, "Did God really say, 'You must not eat from any tree in the garden'?"

- Genesis 3:1 NIV

From the beginning, we have been calling into question, "Did God really say this!?" or "What did He really mean?" Is He trying to withhold good from you? Think about it: have you ever found yourself questioning if God really said something, or meant it the way the Bible clearly teaches? Wondering why God would want to keep something that seemed "good" from you?

Eve already was like God, made in His image. The enemy was convincing her to fight for something that she already obtained.

Convincing Eve of her lacking when she had none. Think on that for a moment. She had everything she needed. She was already made in the image of her Father. She was in relationship with Him- walking and talking in the garden. She had the acceptance, security, significance, authority- she was royalty really. So are we. Yet, we are searching for the significance we already have. You are more than enough. You are made in His image, in His likeness. When we know the nature and goodness of God and realize we are like Him, that is more than enough. When we see His power at work and know that we are able to walk in that same power, life is an unstoppable adventure. When you encounter His gaze at you, His grace towards you, you are forever changed. We find ourselves like Eve, taking a bite of something that is whispering the lie that it will give us something that we already have obtained. Your enemy wants to pile on shame and striving, while your Father has grace and rest for you.

They took the bite, shame entered the scene, they realized they were naked, then they hid. When we are filled with shame, we hide in the shadows. Are there layers of shame in your life that have caused you to hide, to shrink back? He's calling out to you just as He was to them that day in the garden. "Where are you?!?" (Hint: He knows where you are; He just wants you to know He is waiting on you, He is calling you to come...")

"God called to the Man: "Where are you?"
He said, "I heard you in the garden and I was
afraid because I was naked. And I hid." God
said, "Who told you you were naked? Did you
eat from that tree I told you not to eat from?"
- Genesis 3:9-11 NIV

Sister, "Who told you..... ?!?!?" Who told you that you were a failure, that you're not good enough, that you're too much of this and not enough of that? Who told you that you are worthless? Who told you that you had to look a certain way? Who told you that you are incapable of love? Who told you that you would never amount to anything? That you'll never find someone to love you? Who told you.... insert your most common lie, your darkest moments, the accusations that come against you.

When I start to feel lies swarming around me, I always know what will fire me up for the good fight. Recognizing the lie and the source of it is key. Before the truth can set you free, you must realize which lies are holding you hostage. Find the source of the lies, find the entry point and let your Father walk back into the beginning and say, "Who told you?" We don't want to live our lives based on what the father of lies has led us to believe, but we want to follow our heavenly Father to the Way, the Truth and the Life. (John 14:6) There is enmity, open hostility, between us (Genesis 3:15) and the deceiver. God declared war between the serpent and the woman that day and guess what?! We win! I love that infamous Pinterest image that says, "Be the kind of woman that when your feet hit the floor each morning, the devil says, "Oh crap! She's up!"

Are you in? Are you feeling motivated yet on this Monday? Motivated to kick the liar out and walk in the fullness of who you are created to be? I am a firm believer in this: When we see ourselves the way God does, everything changes. When we see ourselves the way God does, our confidence soars and our true beauty is revealed. When we see ourselves the way God does we live lives on purpose, on fire. Talk about "this girl is on fire"-- when you see and walk in the authority and boldness you have as a daughter of the King of Kings, that is fire. Can you imagine life on the other side of this? Walking in confidence that we don't need "acceptance" from anyone because we're already accepted by The One. We don't have to battle daily insecurities, we can walk secure of who we are in Christ. Our search for significance can end when we realize it has already been found. I am who He says I am. Our motivation can be intrinsic rather than extrinsic, simply meaning we can be motivated internally rather than needing the external approval of others all the time. It's this internal strength and knowing that nothing externally can shake. It's not self-confidence, it's GOD-confidence. Confidence isn't being able to say, "they will like me." Confidence is, "I'll be fine if they don't."

"Forget about self-confidence; it's useless. Cultivate God-confidence." - 1 Corinthians 10:12 MSG

Sometimes it's as easy as getting a new pair of glasses, for real. Last year we were about to change jobs, move our family to a new city and embark on a new season of life. This transition caused us to take a look at things differently, quite literally. It was going to be a quick transition and so the hustle was real. We were going to lose our really good health insurance and so as anyone (crazy) would do— you take advantage of all of your benefits in the midst of packing, goodbye parties, and moving. I was in the thick of taking my baby girl to get an MRI, getting my own wisdom teeth pulled (with dry socket drama) and realized I hadn't had an eye exam since I was a little girl. I was always convinced my vision was still perfect 20/20. I figured, while I still had insurance, might as well go check it out.

Immediately, when I started the exam I started laughing out loud, and the examiner probably thought I was insane. I was laughing at how terrible my eyesight was and here I was living my life as if everything was perfect. I didn't know how cloudy things had gotten. Once I slowed down enough to stop and focus on the way I see, I realized it was very messed up! I was also laughing because my husband always told me he thought my vision was bad and I never believed him.

The moral of the story— we're so busy in our daily living that we might not realize that we're not seeing clearly. Our vision of who we are has gotten blurry over time and we may be completely unaware. We may be in need of a **new set of lenses, new vision.**

As little girls we have so much confidence and boldness and slowly, doubt, lies, comparison, negative words-- the world-- starts to cloud the view of ourselves. We've come to accept this awful way of seeing, the distorted lens— as our normal. People around us may even say, "if you could only see what I see"... but we can't. We're stuck, believing "this is the truth, I see it clearly." We may need an examination. Read Psalm 139, one of David's prayers and make it your own.

This is one of my all-time favorite verses, I may say that a million times about every verse— because I just love the Word of God.

[Sidenote, sister: If you ever question what God is saying, why He isn't speaking to you— open this up and ask the Holy Spirit to speak to you. I've had the wildest moments with Him. The kind where you feel it was written thousands of years ago for the moment you're in right this minute.]

"Make a careful exploration of who you are and the work you have been given, and then sink yourself into that. Don't be impressed with yourself. Don't compare yourself with others. Each of you must take responsibility for doing the creative best you can with your own life."
- Galatians 6:4-5 MSG

Let's explore who we are and the work we've been given— and then GO FOR IT! Don't look to the right or the left. Find the personal satisfaction and inner joy of what you discover without allowing comparison to steal a moment of it. Take responsibility, make it your duty, stop waiting for permission from someone else. What lights you up, sets your soul on fire, makes you come alive? You will find your "work," your purpose within that! What are we here for??! To know God and make Him known. What God gave you, it is yours to do so get creative— and do it! Do it differently than you've ever seen, it might not be comfortable or convenient... but the world is waiting for you to be you. You may never know how the path you are pioneering will pave the way for many to find their freedom. It's crucial that we know who we are and what we are living for to keep us on the path to live the full lives we've been promised. Don't settle for less. **You are worth it.**

I AM WORTH IT.

⤜ SOUL WORK:

Your soul work for today sister is to do it: LOOK AT YOU, GIRL. Shut the door, have a private moment-- what do you see? Who is looking back at you? Do you immediately look at your "imperfections" or "flaws"? Are your first feelings divine or filled with disappointment, self-loathing or self-love?

Now invite your Good Father to speak to you. Ask Him what He sees. Start to seek His voice of truth over your sometimes shouting lies,opinions, and critiques. Let Him lead you to seeing yourself the way He does.

If you find yourself struggling, if the lies are swarming like a bunch of bees, buzzing in your ear-- write down, "Who told you?!?!" and put it up somewhere as a reminder. Those lies didn't come from your Father. You are wildly loved.

♫ SONGS:

"Come Alive" by Lauren Daigle
"You Make Me Brave" by Amanda Cook
"No Longer Slaves" by Jonathan & Melissa Helser

Ephesians 1:11
Long before we first heard
of Christ and got our hopes
up, he had his eye on us,
had designs on us for
glorious living, part of the
overall purpose he is
working out in everything
and everyone.

Investigate my life, O God, find out everything about me; Cross–examine and test me, get a clear picture of what I'm about;

See for yourself whether I've done anything wrong— then guide me on the road to eternal life.

Psalm 139

"This means that anyone who belongs to Christ has become a new person. The old life is gone; a new life has begun!"
- 2 Corinthians 5:17 NLT

CHAPTER 2

transformation

CHAPTER TWO

Now that we're motivated to move forward, I'm going to ask you to look back. I know, I know, it seems so anticlimactic. It is so important that we ensure that nothing from our past is still holding unwarranted power over our lives.

The darkness is the devil's playground— what we've kept covered up in the dark, he has the ability to play with. He's swinging with your silence, loving the spiral of your depression down the slide, spinning you in shame, convincing you that your crap is too hard of a climb on the rock wall that you cannot overcome it. Worst of all, you're trapped and alone on this playground with him. He torments us, pushes our buttons on the things unconfessed. In the darkness he can pile on loads of shame and isolation— causing you to believe that you are the "only one", "no one will understand", "you can handle it by yourself".

The moments of pain from our past can stir up so many lies, so much shame, and so much crap that can cloud our true identity. I always liken it to the way it works in our house when someone tells us they're dropping by, or my husband tells me people are coming over and he forgot to tell me. 🙄 What we can get done in a twenty minute power clean I'm convinced is more than we do on a weekly basis of cleaning our house. We get the living room looking impressive, clean the kitchen, make sure the bathroom is as decent smelling as possible (hey, we have three small boys whose aim is not impeccable.) We may even light a candle and put some music on. You know what else we do? We throw a bunch of the stuff we don't want to deal with in "that room" and close the door. "That room" or "that closet" that no one will ever walk in. No one will ever open that door and see that mess. It's the stuff we don't want people to see. It's the crap we say we'll "deal with later". We avoid it at all cost.

"When I refused to confess my sin, my body wasted away, and I groaned all day long."
- Psalm 32:3 NLT

For some of us, just the mention of "that closet"... you know what's in there. You know those moments that marked you, but you'd like to pretend they stay in the past. You may have even said, "I'm taking this to the grave with me, no one will ever know." What I've seen that kind of thinking do is actually dig us into an early grave. Part of us has died or is buried alive suffering with this silenced pain. Shame is that taunting, haunting thing that you find yourself unlovable because of, or think if anyone knew they wouldn't understand. What's hidden haunts you. We'd like to pretend that it's not affecting us— but its effects are wreaking havoc somewhere in our soul. Maybe you're past the pretending-- you know there are issues and you can see some fruit of them in your life, but you have never really dug deeper to know what the root is. It's worth the work to dig, to uncover, to confess and walk in the fullness of freedom and wholeness.

I'm not saying this is a one-stop-shop. It's really

creating a culture in your relationship with self that will not stay satisfied with suffering, with shame, with hiding. Say to yourself, "I'm too amazing to leave myself there." Make the decision— I will uncover, I will expose, I will confess. I will not bury stuff that I deem as dirty— the shame that ends up burying something in me. Remember as David said, his body was wasting away as he kept silent. Create a culture of confession in your life. My friend always says, confess the small things often then there will never be "big things" to confess.

Decide now that you won't make your choices to "save face" (retain respect and avoid potential humiliation) but to always expose where you're at so that you can live a truly whole life. Look at more of Psalm 32 and what David says when he finally decided to let it all out.

"Count yourself lucky, how happy you must be—you get a fresh start, your slate's wiped clean. Count yourself lucky—God holds nothing against you and you're holding nothing back from him. When I kept it all inside, my bones turned to powder, my words became daylong groans. The pressure never let up; all the juices of my life dried up. Then I let it all out; I said, "I'll make a clean breast of my failures to God." Suddenly the pressure was gone— my guilt dissolved, my sin disappeared." - Psalm 32:1-5 MSG

Hold nothing back from Him. I'll say it again: Create a culture of confession in your life. It seems backwards, but isn't most stuff in the kingdom? We always seem to be doing the opposite. The first shall be last; to truly find life, die to self; the greatest shall be the least; to get back at your enemy, love him; to become a great leader, serve; to get rich, give money away; and the list goes on. So it goes with this- to be healed you need to confess that you're sick, that something isn't right or something in the past is still holding you hostage. The Bible says it so well in the book of James:

"Therefore confess your sins to each other and pray for each other so that you may be healed. The prayer of a righteous person is powerful and effective."
-James 5:16 NIV

Confess + pray = healed. I know it's not really a formula, but the part of me that's always looking for them as an easy answer really likes to turn it into one. It brings me hope to know healing is on the other side of confession and prayer. I love how it's followed up by saying the prayer of a righteous person... hold up. I don't think I know any "righteous" people. I kid. When I used to hear righteous, what I really thought was self-righteous, haughty, holier-than-thou — why would I want to confess to that?! That is the last type of person I want to confess my junk to.

Really, a righteous person is simply a person that is morally right or virtuous, very good or excellent. Ah, okay! I can do that. You can do that. Think of the person right now that pops into your mind, ask the Holy Spirit to show you someone righteous and trustworthy that you could take this silent stuff too. It may feel silent now, but what I've learned throughout life is though it may seem harmless and silent now— it's going to come screaming at me sooner or later.

I'll forever remember one of my "cleaning house" moments. Confessing and bringing to the light. It wasn't comfortable or convenient, there were so many cases convincing me in my mind to keep it locked up. "Why do you really need another person?!" But I did it, at 1:00 A.M. I, called my mentor and said, "I need to talk! I know it's late, but I am realizing I need to renounce all of my past sexual encounters." She had me over and we sat on her burgundy couch by the window at 1:00 A.M.. She listened. I confessed. We cried. We prayed. Every backseat moment, dark movie theater or memory from in-between the sheets was brought to the light. The things that would haunt me, that felt horrific to say out loud, I literally felt them lose their power over me as they rolled off my tongue. I knew I was speaking to years of brokenness, of being lost and confused, and I knew that no longer could these moments be held over my head. They were in the light, soul ties broken and renounced of having any power over me. Fun fact is that my mentor then is my mother-in-law now. What we would assume to be the "dirty laundry" we'd never want aired to those closest to us-- literally has zero power and holds no weight in her view of me. Confessing is victory, it is winning. Confession is a weapon against the darkness. He not only forgives us, but He purifies us.

"If we confess our sins, he is faithful and just and will forgive us our sins and purify us from all unrighteousness."
- 1 John 1:9 NIV

The early days of the transformation of Caitlin Crane (my maiden name) felt like it was a story on display for all to see. It was a night and day difference from my first two years of high school to my last two. You see, in the summer months before high school I started training with the girls' basketball team and some of the varsity girls took me under their wing. I had a fast pass to the party scene. So before day one, I had this path set before me. Football season started and my boyfriend cheated on me with a cheerleader. He apologized and wanted to stay together, and my next decision was based on my theology (my belief system) which came from mass media. I immediately thought of the phrase from a song in a current Nike commercial, "Anything you can do, I can do better." It was a taunt between Michael Jordan and Mia Hamm— and it inspired my decision. Sure, we'll stay together... I'll just do it better. I spent the remainder of my freshman and sophomore year as "the party girl", getting drunk and hooking up with random guys each weekend— all while having a boyfriend. I was just "doing it better." I went to a Catholic high school where there was some accountability for your lifestyle after school hours, especially as a student athlete. I already had two strikes— getting caught for showing up to a party drunk and riding with two upperclassmen guy student athletes who were drinking— we were all suspended from spring sports for that. Another strike was that somehow the dean of students found out about a backseat moment with a senior guy— embarrassing, but didn't stop me. I thought I was "on top of the world."

According to my belief system— mass media— all the song lyrics, movies, TV shows— I was living the dream. Invited to every party, wanted by many, living the "popular" life. To truly date me, these were the years before cell phones so my pager was blowing up. A picture I saw played back at our ten year high school reunion, showed the old me pretty perfectly: on the beach in a pink bikini with my pink pager clipped to my side, being held by a guy. I didn't know there was another way. I didn't know what I was missing. Until the summer before my junior year— something happened that would change the course of my life.

That summer I went to a Christian camp with my cousin and 800+ teenagers and no one knew who I was, so my reputation didn't follow. I loved it, I knew I wanted more of God and I wanted to experience what I watched others encountering. One evening service the preacher was doing something that I had no clue what it was— but I could tell it was real. He had called two people out of the crowd of 800+ and was basically "reading their mail" so to speak. He was speaking truth into them and saying things that a stranger simply could not know about your life. I remember seeing the realness of God in that moment, knowing heaven was speaking. A big "jock" guy was bawling as this stranger told him about his life and what God was speaking into his future. I stood there and said, "God, if you're real and you want me to give you my life, to leave my friends and "popularity"... have that man call me up there." Before I could finish that prayer in my mind— he pointed me out of the crowd and said, "girl in the black v-neck shirt." The words that were spoken next were perfectly fitting about everything in that season— then he spoke of the "power" on my life... a moment I will truly never forget. The theme of that summer camp was "No Looking Back, No Going Back, No Way" and I didn't. I was saved that day and never looked back.

The next two years of high school looked entirely different. I began leading the campus ministry at my school, I led the "Live Jesus" retreat, became a student leader at youth group, and was bringing friends by the carload to church. I remember hearing rumors of guys saying they didn't want Caitlin any more because "she's going to become a nun." Ha. I became Senior Class President and launched a Senior-led Freshmen Retreat that would share with incoming freshmen that "there is another way." I remember thinking, "if only I knew then what I know now." Don't you have those moments? Here's the thing: you can pay it forward to a little sister. Be who you needed when you were younger. Start something that will leave a legacy in place of the pain you experienced. Do something that your younger self would be thankful for. Here's my story on the other side of this. This summer I had the honor of visiting my old high school in Florida, sixteen years later. The Freshmen Retreat is still going strong and impacting the lives of brand new high school students. I was able to sit in the crowd and hear a senior girl, named Megan, drop some wisdom on these fresh students that I want to share with you today. Let these truths not only speak to you but show you the power of transformation and rewriting the story:

> *"Be unapologetically yourself. You bring something unique to the world, remain true to who you are. There is too little time in life to work hard to be someone else. Ignore stereotypes. You lose yourself when you give in to social pressure. Be the best version of yourself. Pray. Write your own story."*

After hearing stories and witnessing the sixteen years of students get to write their own story with an entirely different message I was just blown away. I was able to share the last talk that night with the crowd of students. To tell them my story of transformation and to please hear from the "big sister" who wish she would've known a different path. That it's worth it. To make the maybe "unpopular" choice to stay free-- and that life with Jesus was really the most rewarding, adventurous life. In closing I shared this,

"Don't copy the behavior and customs of this world, but let God transform you into a new person by changing the way you think. Then you will learn to know God's will for you, which is good and pleasing and perfect."
- Romans 12:2 NLT

One encounter can change everything, not only for you-- but for those to follow the new trail you blaze. Your life story could be the survival guide to someone else's trek up the mountain. Keep blazing, keep pursuing wholeness and laying hold of the full life, the life of freedom that Christ gave His life for. In order to do this you need to walk it out and share it, leave a path. Own your story and let it bring God glory. Own it, every part. Sometimes we keep parts hidden that the enemy would love to let silence and shame win, but Jesus' blood really does break every chain and make all things new. I believe wholeheartedly in not allowing the enemy of my soul to "own" any part of my past. Jesus' life and sacrifice on the cross was "enough", more than enough really, to pay for it all. To redeem it, to restore it, to rewrite it.

There was one thing that for years I'd never shared. So much of my story was in the spotlight for all to see, being a youth pastor and sharing it with many. Until God spoke to me so sweetly about something that I'd kept hidden. He's so sweet and He didn't do it in a way to expose me, but in a way to show His love and grace in such a powerful display. We were leading the response time at a youth conference full of teenagers. I felt God say something to me that out of His kindness brought another memory out of shame and into the light of truth. My senior year, during a school dance one of my guy friends said he wanted to show me something. He called into the boys' bathroom in the freshmen wing to make sure no one was inside. He led me into the stall and I saw my name engraved with a terrible statement on the stall. It filled me with shame and embarrassment in the moment and that moment stayed locked up like a vault. I told no one for years. Until the Lord so sweetly reminded me of this and said,

"Your name was engraved on the boys' bathroom stall, and now it is engraved on my hands."

Talk about transformation. No matter how "big" or "small" your need for change may feel, He is more than capable. C.S. Lewis said "Jesus didn't come to make bad people good, but to make dead people live." It's not simply about changing some behavior— it's about changing your beliefs. Remember, when we see ourselves the way God does, everything changes. There are parts of you that are lying dormant, that have been buried deep, but we have the resurrection power. He wants to call you back to life. He wants to resurrect your hope, your ability to dream and to make sure you're living in the freedom He paid such a high price for. Remember those dreams you had as a little girl-- the childlike crazy faith, when we feel unstoppable— that is real. We are unstoppable with Him. When I tell the story of my transformation, I feel like I'm telling the story of a girl I saw in a movie. Which always reminds me of how the Bible says,

---

Psalm 103:12 NLT
"He has removed our sins as far from us as the east is from the west."

I got a fresh start, my old life is gone. I am thriving in my new life. I truly am a new creation. Regardless of how colorful your past was, or how close it still feels, forgiveness and freedom are just on the other side of receiving it. We must learn to see past our past. What you've done does not define you. Your past does not dictate your future. No reputation is stronger than His redemption. Even if you feel stuck in a part of your story that seems never-ending, an endless cycle of pain, He can literally transform anything. Rather than focus so much on transforming your outside with more makeup, clothes, filters, let's truly believe with Him we can be transformed from the inside out. I want to take care of my character before my appearance. Nothing from your past is allowed to hold unwarranted power over your life. Create a culture of confession in your life today. Who's your righteous person? Open the door to that room where you might have stuffed your junk you don't want to deal with, the stuff you've kept silent about. Don't stay silent. Confess + pray= be healed. Take a moment, send a text, make a phone call, have a 1:00 A.M. couch session— do whatever it takes, because as His daughter:

You are forgiven + free. You are new.

your name here

I AM FORGIVEN
+ FREE.
I AM NEW.

SOUL WORK:

What have you stuffed in "that room" that you don't want to deal with?

Text or call your "righteous" person that you can confess to. Create the culture of confession in your own life.

Own your story and let it bring God glory. If you never have, write out your story or share it with someone.

SONGS:

"Out of Hiding" by Steffany Gretzinger
"How Can It Be" by Lauren Daigle
"Defender" by Upper Room Music
"Open Up Let the Light In" by Steffany
        Gretzinger
"Letting Go" by Steffany Gretzinger

"Words kill, words give life;
they're either poison or
fruit-- you choose."
- Proverbs 18:21 MSG

CHAPTER 3

Wednesday

CHAPTER THREE

Happy **WORD** Wednesday girls! There is so much about this day of the week that I hope we can dive into together and really go after. I'm believing our "coffee chat" today will be something that sticks and changes the way we look at the power of our words. Without a doubt, words are powerful-- whether they're written down and read or spoken words that are heard, they become thoughts that linger or labels that really stick. They hold the power of life and death inside of them. Today we're going to look at what words we're carrying with us on the daily. Our words create worlds. Isn't that wild? The words we speak create the reality we live in. The words we hear and accept as truth, become our beliefs and eventually our behaviors. So I don't know if you've seen the movie, "Mean Girls", but one of the silly statements from it that is now showing up on T-Shirts and Instagram squares is, "On Wednesdays we wear pink." That phrase and concept has been adopted by many, but regardless of whether pink is your color or not... I'd like to steal the phrase and upgrade it a bit to: "On Wednesdays we wear pink, and watch what we think."

Why does it seem easier to find words of death, words that kill our confidence? Our dreams? Our hope? It seems these words that kill something inside of us stick so much easier. Think about a time someone has said something negative to you or about you and how easy it is for that thought to stick.

Yet when someone calls out the gold in us, compliments us or speaks life into us-- it can be so easy to shrug it off and make excuses for it. "You just have to say that" or "they're just being nice". It's been proven that we need about five positive words spoken for every one negative word. I want to be a woman who speaks words of life, and I want to uproot all of the poisonous words that have taken root in my mind. It's difficult for us to see ourselves the way God does when we have so many other words blaring at us as if through a loudspeaker, written on our forehead, or attached to our name wherever we go. Obviously, those are all metaphors, but they can feel all too real at times.

"Sticks and stones may break my bones, but words can never hurt me."

What a classic way we were taught as kids to protect ourselves from words— yet, how untrue. "Words can never hurt me." I remember saying this line with the typical "nah nah boo boo" type ring to it in defense of all of my emotions, pain, and heartache. If you think back to your childhood, can you remember negative words that were spoken to or about you? Maybe by classmates, by bullies, written words on notes passed or online, a reputation or story told about you that seemed unshakeable. Maybe they were words spoken by people you loved and who did love you, but were simply not aware of the power of their words in their moment of frustration or pain. Words in your head that you'd never speak out loud feel like they carry so much weight that they harass you. For me, the word I always remember that for some reason carried so much embarrassment was when a boy in seventh grade called me a "chameleon". When I actually speak it out or even now, write it down, it seems so crazy that that one statement felt so full of shame and embarrassment. I struggled hardcore with terrible skin and acne and I remember thinking he was talking about my face. The first thing I thought of when I heard chameleon, is skin that changes colors-- of course I thought he was talking about my skin and how red and bumpy it was. It wasn't until this year, when I learned more about my personality, that I had a crazy revelatory moment and realized that he was most likely talking about my behavior and not my appearance. A chameleon is someone who changes their opinions or behavior according to their situation. I naturally applied 'chameleon' to the area of my life that I was the most insecure about and then it was as if I subconsciously added so much more power to it. It is a pretty perfect picture of how focused I was on my outer appearance rather that what's inside. What about you? Can you take a moment and think about a negative word or statement you've believed about yourself that you need to find the root to? It's okay to admit the hurt of the word-- the power of the word-- and then we get to uproot the ones that don't belong in our beautiful minds.

We get to choose what words and what thoughts live in our minds and impact our lives. Just because we have a thought, does not mean it belongs to us. Some words have been spoken to us or said about us and have dug themselves so deep that they now infiltrate our thoughts often. Instead of pointing it out as unhealthy, a toxic thought or a lie, we began to accept that word and we adopted it as our own. We begin to think on these words as if they originated inside of us and are a part of who we truly are. We choose whether to accept or reject those thoughts, those words. When they're coming at you from someone else and they are not truth-based, you have the power to reject them.

"I'm not going to walk around on eggshells worrying about what small-minded people might say. I'm going to stride free and easy, knowing what our large minded Master has already said."
- 1 Corinthians 10:29 MSG

Isn't that so good? So often we do just that, walk around on eggshells constantly caring what people think. We do not live for the approval of man; we belong to God. When we see ourselves the way He does, with His truth constantly on our mind, we will be able to stand firmly in who we are. Words can be labels over our minds eye that greatly affect our perspective. The Bible says,

"...as a woman thinks in her heart, so is she."
- Proverbs 23:7 NKJV *(female emphasis added)*

The words you believe about yourself become who you are. We live out the labels we've put on ourselves or received from others. You are what you think. So, we're going to take a moment here to pause. The title of this book is, "Look at You, Girl." You may have wondered if you're supposed to be looking at yourself, why the lashes with the closed eyes?! Why wouldn't the eyes be open to see? I sincerely had a revelation, a moment with the Lord, where He told me: "I want my girls to look at themselves from the inside out. You are going to teach them to look inside first and not be distracted by anything on the outside." Isn't that amazing? Let's adopt this practice as our own. Let's see ourselves from the inside out, with the foundation of what God has said about us first.

"The LORD doesn't see things the way you see them. People judge by outward appearance, but the LORD looks at the heart."
- 1 Samuel 16:7 NLT

Let's do a heart check. Rather than assessing ourselves by how we're doing externally-- maybe that would be your grades, your income, your follower count, your fitness level, your outer beauty-- whatever that may be, let's look inside at our thought life and check if it's healthy. To get started, doodle some of the first words of lies, labels and love (the good stuff, too!) that you think about yourself. What are the first words that come to mind that you have believed are at the core of you? Write them down-- the good, the bad, the ugly. There is no shame in this, we are going to look at them for what they are and then allow God to speak the truth to us and also learn the power we have to kick out the lies and begin to truly believe and walk in truth and love. Go ahead, write them in the margins of the page or grab a scrap paper or journal take a moment here and now to do this before you continue reading.

LOOK AT YOU, GIRL

(close your eyes, look inside out... write it down)

Now, here is the good news: we have the power of the living God inside of us, therefore we are powerful. You have the power to choose the words that rattle around in your head, the labels that you have in your mind's eye, the statements that ultimately define you. Those words, those labels— they become our identity. You are what you believe. When we take time to stop and question what we believe to be true about ourselves, we realize the foundation is often found full of lies, outside pressures, performance-based thinking, popularity-seeking, trying to fit in; we never feel comfortable in our own skin or have yet to discover who we actually are. Now, I'm not saying I've arrived— I'm not sure there is a final destination this side of eternity. It's definitely an adventurous journey, and I believe that this journey should be full of joy in discovering how our Daddy made us, uniquely, not trying to fit in a mold or model our life after someone else's design. I actually did an Instagram poll and then collected tons of DMs about what the lies are that you most often believe about yourself or have overcome in your life. I typed out this extremely long list of all of the lies and stupid accusations from the enemy of our souls. As I read over them, I found that the most common lies or root beliefs in the lie came down to one of two things:

The root of most lies
we believe about ourselves:
I'm not enough.
I'm too much.

Isn't that crazy? But it's the root of what so many of us struggle with on the daily. I'm not good enough, smart enough, pretty enough, funny enough, bold enough OR the antithesis is I'm way too much for people— too loud, too weird, too raw, too quiet, too open, or too private.

The truth is so foreign because the lies are so familiar. We are bombarded daily with the lies— based on the words of others, the billboards we pass by on our daily drive, the social media scrolling screaming at us, the opinions of everyone else. As girls we face an onslaught daily with a whole bunch of "shoulds" targeting us. Things like: you should be a size two, you should have long beach-wavy curls, you should wear these expensive shoes, you should listen to this music, you should do this to attract a guy, you should act like this to be liked, you should have this nice purse-- the shoulds seem to never stop. The words that sling at us what kind of girl we "should" be. It takes so much intentionality to find the truth and know who we are meant to be, who we are in Christ. Let these next words bring you hope:

"It's in Christ that we find out who we are and what we are living for."
- Ephesians 1:11 MSG

We get to "turn up truth" in our lives. Figuratively, we need to turn down the volume to the lies and turn up the volume to truth. This takes being super intentional since the lies are so easily accessible. It takes guarding our eyes, our ears, our minds and going after the truth we find in the Word. We need to know what He says. When you feel lost and don't know what way to go, when you can't tell what is truth and what is a lie, when you feel unsure about life in general... be comforted in knowing that you have access to "the Way, the Truth, and the Life". (John 14:6 NIV) When you can, have a quiet moment and read all of chapter 14 in the gospel of John, it is so full of hope and the powerful promises of Jesus. So here's the thing, you can find out who you are in Christ by asking Him and by reading His gift of words to us. I don't know where you're at right now with your personal view and relationship with the Word of God. I don't know if maybe even that feels like a "should" in your life, an "oh crap, I should be reading my Bible more." Maybe you feel completely lost about where to start or what the point is. I want to share with you my experience, that will hopefully encourage you no matter where you are with it. The Word of God is UHHHH-MAZZZ-ING! I am telling you something, it is ALIVE and ACTIVE, for real.

"For the word of God is alive and active. Sharper than any double-edged sword, it penetrates even to dividing soul and spirit, joints and marrow; it judges the thoughts and attitudes of the heart."
- Hebrews 4:12 NIV

I have had so many moments in my life, sometimes that felt so "dry and weary", lifeless, hopeless, where I didn't "feel anything" from God and then He used His word to speak right to me. Moments where the words seem to jump off of the page like they had been written thousands of years ago just for me. As if, no one else would ever read them. It really is His love letter to us. It judges the thoughts and attitudes of our hearts. The Bible is the greatest gift that we take for granted. If you haven't had this experience, or it's been awhile, ask Him to speak to you through His word. Just ask. Just wait on Him to do something so special. There were seasons I would literally stay up all night in my bedroom reading His word, there were other times I needed it so bad I'd sleep with it under my pillow. His word is our lifeline. It is our source of life and hope and truth. Especially in the current state of our world and even the Christian world at times-- opinions outside of the Word seem to be blaring. We need to be rooted in His word. It's not a shamey-should, it's an exciting-- wow! What adventure and life will I encounter today. I once heard it said, "if we want revival-- we need a return to the Bible." Not growing up in the church, I've never had a frame of reference for "revival" necessarily, but I know we need a return to the Bible. After simply googling the definition of revival, you find: "an improvement in the condition or strength of something; an instance of something becoming popular, active or important again." Yes, we need an improvement in the condition and strength of our spirits and our souls. We need the truth to become important again. Another definition says, "an often highly emotional evangelistic meeting or series of meetings." I'm not sure it necessarily needs to look like that, but a "spiritual awakening"? Yes, please. A revival of your life, a reawakening. It can and will come through the word of God. The Bible isn't old news, it's the Good News. The Good News that we need in our body, soul and spirit every day. The words He has been speaking over us from the beginning of time hold more weight than anything else if we only let them. Ask the Lord, "what are your thoughts toward me?" Give yourself quiet space alone with him to slow down and listen.

"For I know the thoughts I think toward you, says the Lord, thoughts of peace and not of evil, to give you a future and a hope."
- Jeremiah 29:11 NKJV

"Your eyes saw my substance, being yet
unformed. And in Your book they all were
written, the days fashioned for me, when as yet
there were none of them. How precious also are
Your thoughts to me, O God! How great is the
sum of them!"
- Psalm 139:16-17 NKJV

Now is the fun part. The process of exchanging the
truth for the lies. I like to call it, "the great
exchange." I know I've been talking over and over
about the fact that we get to choose, to accept or
reject the thoughts that are coming at us, the words
about us. After you've heard from the Lord of what
he thinks-- let's find what lies and thoughts we've
been thinking that are obviously not from Him, that
don't line up with what He has to say and replace
them. The reason I call this, "the great exchange" is
because in the book of Romans it talks about how
they did just the opposite:

"They exchanged the truth about God for a lie,
and worshiped and served created things
rather than the Creator."
- Romans 1:25 NIV

Let's flip this and kick the lies out-- and fill our
minds with truth. Here are some of the most
beautiful truths found in the Word about who we are.

You are loved.   You are an overcomer.
You are worthy.   You are gifted.
You are forgiven.   You are an heiress.
You are powerful.   You have a purpose.
You are free.   You are capable.

You are not your past.
You are enough.
You are not anxious.
You are not afraid.
You are full of joy.
You are accepted.
You are strong.
You are secure.

You are a conqueror.
You are not alone.
You are loyal.
You overcome.
You have authority.
You have a voice.
You are an original.
You are set apart.

YOU HAVE THE MIND OF CHRIST.

These can be declarations you speak over yourself. They are strong and powerful words that have references in the Bible. (You can find an entire list of these identity scriptures and references in the back of this book.) The replacing part is so important, when you have a negative thought-- a lie or a label-- it can be hard to stop thinking on it. I liken it to the idea of saying, "okay, stop thinking about the pink elephant." Immediately my mind pictures a pink elephant. Rather than say to stop thinking about the pink elephant, I need to replace it with another thought. Here are plenty of powerful truths about who you are in Christ that can replace the lies that have probably lived in your head for too long. Speak God's Word over yourself until you've changed your own mind and heart. This is what it means to "take thoughts captive" and to replace them with truth. I love this verse that serves as such a pep-talk reminder of how powerful we are as children of God.

"For though we live in the world, we do not wage war as the world does. The weapons we fight with are not the weapons of the world. On

the contrary, they have divine power to demolish strongholds. We demolish arguments and every pretension that sets itself up against the knowledge of God, and we take captive every thought to make it obedient to Christ."
- 2 Corinthians 10:3-5 NIV

Your words are weapons that wage war. Guess what, sis? You win! We have the victory, we do not need to live as victims to the onslaught of lies and negative words around us. Let's build a new world to live in with our words. Let's change the trajectory of our lives with our self-talk. Our self-talk should be infused with scriptural truth daily. I love how Lisa Bevere said, "Talk to yourself like you would to someone you love." What do you say about yourself? If you want to know what you think about yourself, listen to what you say about yourself. We have this strange dynamic where it almost feels wrong to think well of ourselves, it's like we have this built-in insecurity that says there is no way we could be enough.

What are your top three favorite things about yourself? Why does that feel so hard to come up with, how sad is that!? If you don't like what you're saying, you need to look at what you're thinking. Tell yourself the truth, preach to yourself. I love doing this, "you are a wonder woman, you are strong, you are capable, your husband is madly in love with you, your kids think you're the best, you walk in authority, people see God through your life." Change your inner language, hear from God and speak it out. Replace careless words like, "I'm so stupid," "I'm too lazy," "I'm the worst at..." You are brilliant, God did not mess up on you. In your weakness, He is strong.

Fill up on truth.

Listen, this book is written for us to take a look at ourselves and this chapter more specifically about the words we think, speak and believe about ourselves. I simply cannot finish this chapter in good conscious when writing a book for females and about words and not "go there" with the gossip conversation. I know this may seem a bit stereotypical, but this very conversation is so important to make sure that we are being true to ourselves and loving our sisters well. Sisters, is the first word to focus on. When we change our perspective from "that girl", whether she's that girl who's annoying, loud, mean, rude, distant, hurt me, hurt someone I love, the one who has it all together or the one you just wish your life was more like. It's high time we embrace each other as sisters. One of my favorite hashtag beliefs I made up in my head (you do that too, right?) is #strangerstosisters I always joke that I could have a thirty minute coffee with someone and we could go from strangers to sisters, just like that. We are more careful with our words when we realize these are our sisters who have their own stories, so let's watch our words about them. So let's just look at THE Word first. It makes it pretty simple. Watch the way you talk. Say only what HELPS, our words are supposed to be gifts to one another.

"Watch the way you talk. Let nothing foul or dirty come out of your mouth. Say only what helps, each word a gift."
- Ephesians. 4:29 MSG

"It only takes a spark, remember, to set off a

forest fire. A careless or wrongly placed word
out of your mouth can do that. By our speech
we can ruin the world, turn harmony to
chaos, throw mud on a reputation, send the
whole world up in smoke and go up in smoke
with it, smoke right from the pit of hell."
-James 3:5-6 MSG

Don't be careless with your words. One tip I used to
tell our girls at summer camp, because for some
reason gossip would historically run rampant there,
was to "put on your chapstick", watch the words
coming out of your mouth. The best thing about this
simple illustration is in those awkward moments
when a friend is starting to speak negatively about
someone, you can gently remind them to choose
better by reminding them to use their chapstick.
Make a commitment to yourself and within your
friendships to watch your words. Here is a really
simple tool that helps you to think before you speak:

Before you speak, THINK:
-Is is True?
-Is it Helpful?
-Is it Inspiring?
-Is it Necessary?
-It is Kind?

So there it is, let's resolve to kick out the lies that
don't belong in your beautiful mind, you are
powerful to choose what you become based on what
you believe. Commit to watch your words-- that
you speak to yourself and to and about others. Your
words carry the power of life and death.

I AM POWERFUL.

𝄞 SOUL WORK:

Write down the labels and lies that you refuse to accept, tear them up & trash them.

Circle the top five truths listed that you need to make your own. Find the biblical references for them in the back of the book and underline them in your Bible.

Do a Google search on the Bible and gossip.

♫ SONGS:

"You Say" by Lauren Daigle
"Who You Say I Am" by Hillsong
"All He Says I Am" by Cody Carnes
"I Am No Victim" by Kristene Dimarco

Ephesians 4:29 MSG
"Watch the way you talk. Let nothing foul or dirty come out of your mouth. Say only what helps, each word a gift."

"We will not compare ourselves with each other as if one of us were better and another worse.
We have far more interesting things to do with our lives.
Each of us is an original."
- Galatians 5:26 MSG

CHAPTER 4

thankfully

CHAPTER FOUR

You are an original. There is no one that is you, that is your power. There are specific and unique things about your makeup that no one else has or ever has had. Today we're going to figure out how to be thankful for our uniqueness. We will learn to choose gratitude over criticism and comparison.

What happens when you look in a mirror? Do you immediately think loving, truth-filled, good thoughts or do you automatically get filled with feelings of disgust, perfectionism or terrible thoughts about yourself? Simply put, do you have positive or negative thoughts and feelings when you see yourself? Stop with me and think about how crazy it is that as women, young and old, we are sold the lie that we have to fix our "problem areas." What a ridiculous idea that an entire industry is targeting and telling us what is "wrong" about our face or our body. Sister, there is nothing inherently wrong with you. Your beauty comes from within and will glow from the inside out when your soul is healthy. Instead we're bombarded with lies like your nose is too big, your legs are too skinny, your face is too round, your hair isn't the right color, your lips are too thin, your eyebrows aren't the right shape, and the list goes on. When we were younger, it's that something is too big or too small, stuff this or suck that in. As we grow older it becomes all about the laugh lines or "crow's feet". I'm pretty sure there are no bird's feet on my face and as I age I will celebrate the lines that show I've lived a life full of laughter and joy. I'm not saying we don't take care of ourselves— our bodies are a temple of the Holy Spirit and should be treated well. I'm simply suggesting there is more to self-care than face masks and hair treatments. I'm wondering if we could get our soul healthy enough that we could truly be thankful for who we are and how we've been designed - on purpose with purpose.

The core message of "Look at You, Girl" with the lashes as our symbol is to present the idea of looking from the inside out. Starting with eyes closed, looking internally at what we are made up of and moving outward from there. What is our character, our values, our passion, our personality, our own fire-- before we look at the external. We will dig more into how to like what you see when you look inside on Saturday. Today, I want us to go after what happens when we look in the mirror. When you look in the mirror, what do you see? I remember seeing this image on social media of a little note taped to a mirror saying: "Warning: reflections in this mirror may be distorted by socially constructed ideas of beauty." That is very true, the mirror can be a dangerous place if we haven't been taught how to love ourselves well. Let's eradicate this "standard of beauty" and distorted views on it. One thing I find so deep, is that this standard makes it so that everyone wants to look the same. Same hair color, length, style, eyebrow shape, eyelashes, cheek bones, lip size, the list goes on. Our beauty is in our uniqueness. You are an original. There is no one just like you. Beautiful does not mean everyone looks the same, it celebrates our differences.

A few years ago, I was sharing a message with

hundreds of girls at a youth conference. I used this visual illustration that really helped the message sink in for me and for them. I want to share it with you. Fun fact, I actually preached this message nine months pregnant and in four-inch heels, that's just how I roll. Ha. So now you can picture this story with that image. I talked about what happens when we look in a mirror. On stage was a massive mirror that almost doubled me in size. As soon as I saw myself in the mirror, I wrote all over it words some of us think right away. "Ugly." "Not enough." "Shame." What would the lies and labels be that you have heard or come to believe about yourself? Labels that either define you or come to suck the life out of you. Lots of what we talked about yesterday or things we just pick apart about our physical appearance. Some of my first glance thoughts about myself would be things like terrible skin, wide face, no boobs, double chin, fluffy tummy, and so on. Lies about the internal views like used goods, not enough, fraud, let someone else do it, etc. I taught about how the view we see in the mirror is typically fueled by the outside world, not by the truth of who God says we are. Then we declared, "enough is enough" as I took out a hammer and smashed the mirror to pieces. As it shattered and I probably was coincidentally shocking the crowd, we had this massive eleven foot cross being erected on the opposite side of the stage. The cross was covered in a beautiful mosaic of mirror pieces. This was a visual illustration and dream I'd had for years, I had done it on a small scale in my core group years before.

If you can imagine with me for a moment, it's time we take out the hammer and shatter the way the world tells us to see ourselves. It is okay to get mad enough to have your own, "enough is enough" moment with the lies that assault you every time you look in the mirror. I wouldn't recommend taking a hammer to it, but maybe a proverbial one. Identify the negative thoughts, their roots, and kick them out. The dream is that we could see ourselves the way He does so that when we look in the mirror we don't see our "problem areas" and a completely distorted view of beauty. We get to see ourselves authentically and be thankful for this life we've been given. I wish I could meet you where you sit with this book right now and have a massive mosaic mirror cross in front of you. He changed everything on that cross for us. The most powerful display of radical love for us there on the cross. When I get "stuck" in my self-stuff, one thing that always helps me to get out, to get free is to remember the cross. When I act like my stuff is "so big", it's like I'm saying "the cross wasn't enough." Sister, we walk in freedom because of that cross, we have all authority given to us because of His resurrection. You have resurrection power living on the inside. So let's refuse to let the world's mirror win another day and be set on the gaze of Jesus. To look in the mirror and smile as He is so happy with how you are made, from the inside out. His word says,

"You are altogether beautiful, my darling; there is no flaw in you".
- Song of Solomon 4:7 NIV

"You are God's masterpiece."
- Ephesians 2:10 NLT

Stop being so hard on the girl in the mirror. Instead of the mirror being a place of unrelenting critiques, make it a space to see God's relentless love for the masterpiece He made. What would happen if every time we saw a mirror our mind was triggered to think of one simple, but powerful word: thankful. I believe it would revolutionize our mindset and perspective. I think we'd begin to let gratitude kill every layer of discontentment. I think truth would fill our view and the lies would be kicked out. Let's try it. Grab your old lipstick, a dry erase marker, a sticky note, whatever works and write "thankful" on your mirror. Remember yesterday how we talked about the fact that we have the ability to change our thoughts? Let's retrain our brain when we see a mirror. Let's tell our mind to be kind every time we see or say something about ourselves. So here's the new normal when we see a mirror: "I'm thankful inside and out." Think of something you see that you're thankful for and something beyond what you can see. It can be hard for some of us to think of things we like about ourselves because there have been large mental pathways (remember the highways we talked about yesterday) paved in our mind that have believed the bad things. I'll say it again, the truth is so foreign because the lies are so familiar. We have to turn up the truth. The truth is there is a long list of amazing things about you, inside and out. In case you're feeling stuck and can't think of much, which is sad but okay, we're learning. Here's some examples from my social media poll:

I'm thankful for my creative solutions and my long silky hair.
I'm thankful for my heart to serve others and my big smile.
I'm thankful for my deep brown eyes and my hunger to live life to its fullest capacity.

I'm thankful for my freckles and my commitment to tell the truth in love.
I'm thankful for my green eyes and my ability to make people laugh.

Are you in? Are you ready to tell your mind to be kind, and create your new normal when you see a mirror? Let's set ourselves up for good triggers that bring to light the most important things. Let's celebrate who we are and what we've been given. Fall in love with Who made you and His good design. He made you from the inside out and called it good, believe it.

Pause here and make your first new mirror moment happen. If you're all snuggled up with the book and don't want to get up- grab your phone, it is probably close by. Put that thing on selfie mode and take a look, smile at yourself, say hello, think of what you're thankful for inside and out.

I hope this is just the beginning of refusing to speak down to or about yourself, to love yourself well and see the daughter of a King looking back in the mirror. It is so freeing to know and be reminded that we get to change our mindsets when they're stuck in negative pathways. We get to celebrate our strengths, our gifts. Have you ever taken a personality test that you felt hit the nail on the head? I personally love personality tests, though I understand not one of them is complete or the end-all to who I am. But it constantly gives me new language and appreciation for a part of myself. It helps me recognize the way I tick, some of the why and teaches me to be thankful for how God made me rather than trying to be like "her" or "them". One of my favorites is "Strengths Finder." I love this book and test because it helps you identify what your strengths are and encourages you to continue to complain about your weaknesses - celebrate who you are rather than focus on what you are not.

Meet Jenna, she is fun and free-spirited; she has strengths of connectedness and empathy. Even though she is extremely lovable and is surrounded by people who think the world of her, she is constantly discontent. She struggles with self-hatred and feeling like she never measures up. She is always looking to her two friends she grew up with. One friend, Melissa, is on the fast track to being a doctor. She is so good in school, aces every test with little effort and is so prim and proper. Her other friend, Tanya, is simply stunning. Every room she walks into the eyes go to her. She is a show stopper and can sing like it's her job. Actually, it probably will be one day. She just got invited to record a demo. Then there's Jenna, who has the inner makeup of a

Mother Teresa/Oprah mix. Her gifts and strengths could change the world but she doesn't know herself. She's looking at her blaring weaknesses and thinking she'll never be good at anything. She struggles to get a B on a test and can't sing a lick. Even her little cousins give her a side eye when she's singing "Happy Birthday" out of tune. So what's a girl to do? She looks around and feels like she cannot measure up. She is never taught to look inside and see her own strength. She feels stuck. Her friends and parents think, "Jenna, if only you could see yourself the way we do."

Does this story sound familiar at all? Maybe it's your own complicated story or that of a loved one? This is why these tools can be so helpful. There are a few good options to look into: Strengths Finder, Enneagram, Meyers-Briggs, the Five Love Languages, and more. Research that helps give language to who you are from the inside out and how you best give and receive love. Have you ever read something before and thought, "wow, that's what I always think, but didn't know how to say it?!" There are lots of resources out there for you if you're not sure what your "gifts" are. You have something unique to bring to your world, celebrate it and give thanks.

"The fastest way to kill something special is to compare it to something else." - Anonymous

As soon as you have this special moment or maybe even a complete perspective shift the enemy of your soul would love for nothing else to come in and steal that immediately, inciting your eyes to look at someone else. Just like Jenna who couldn't see the gold in herself because her eyes were so stuck on the gifts of those around her. Comparison is an ugly enemy to godly self-acceptance. It causes us to not see ourselves the way He does, full of gratitude and empowerment, but rather to measure ourselves by someone else's standards. We get so stuck looking at someone else's gifts that we take our own for granted. We make a long list of our shortcomings or how we should be more or less of "this" and "that". Rather than being thankful for the way we are made, we think we need to be more of "that" and less of "this". We think "well, she is so 'that'" and "look at her, I'm stuck being too much like 'this.'"

"To be nobody but yourself in a world which is doing it's best, night and day, to make you everybody but yourself— means to fight the hardest battle which any human being can fight and never stop fighting."
- E.E. Cummings

Okay, hold up. You may be thinking, this is "Thankful Thursday" so why on earth did we just switch the subject to comparison? Comparison steals our gratitude. It turns our grateful attitude into a jealous, envious, bitter attitude. Comparison stirs up discontent with who you are, what you have and what you do. So we are going to spend some time digging into this subject and uprooting the lies of what "comparison" truly is. I believe when we do this, we will be set free to live more thankful, joy-filled, purpose driven lives.

I like to call it the comparison trap, it is so easily talked about and owned by myself and so many of us. I realized it's a really pretty label on something really ugly. I feel like it's easy for me to say, "Yes. I struggle with comparison." But what is really behind the door of comparison? Jealousy, envy, bitterness, pride, and the list of nasty just goes on. I have always agreed with the thought that, "recognizing the problem is half the battle." Well if this is true, then mislabeling the problem is a major issue. I can say, "oh I just need to stop comparing," and move on with my day. But when I open the door of comparison, I must realize what's behind that door and in my heart is a whole lot of jealousy over my perceived notions of what others get to do; envy of what others have that I don't think they deserve (or if they do, then I definitely do); bitterness towards others or God for not "blessing" me with "that"; pride that I am so much better than someone who made that bad choice. I mean all kinds of evil really.

"For wherever there is jealousy and selfish ambition, there you will find disorder and evil of every kind."
- James 3:16 NLT

What a word of truth. So if the comparison in my life is stirring up jealousy, envy and selfish ambition... I can know what will follow: disorder, confusion, every kind of evil. No wonder it can "seep into every area" of my life or seem to consume my thoughts at times. It's a disorder I don't want to dive into. I picture a trap door in the floor; the trap being comparison. Once I fall into the trap, I'm swimming in the mess of pride, jealousy, envy, bitterness, and more.

I'm pretty sure this has happened since the Stone Ages, but in our time of social media, it's on steroids. The comparison trap is at our fingertips all day long.

We can get into a daze as we scroll through others' lives instead of appreciating our own. Watch your thoughts while you scroll, as I often say: slow your scroll. Pay attention to what is feeding and fueling your thoughts. Are you feeling any envy, bitterness, pride, jealousy, self-loathing, competition? If so, take a break. Hit that unfollow button if that feed isn't feeding your soul anything good. If it is sending you on a downward spiral, stop it. *[Sidenote sister, there are loads of accounts you can follow that are filled with daily encouragement and truth. People who are aiming to inspire, not just impress. Feeds full of truth and scripture. Find those and follow. Stop subscribing to accounts that don't line up with your most treasured values and the path you want to be on.]*

I'm going to share my "gratitude game" I made up for myself. If I'm scrolling and start to feel myself getting stuck, I stop. I go to my own feed and scroll. It it impossible for me not to count my blessings and be filled with gratitude for my beautiful life.

"Look after each other so that none of you fails to receive the grace of God. Watch out that no poisonous root of bitterness grows up to trouble you, corrupting many."
- Hebrews 12:15 NLT

Let's make sure that we're not allowing the poison of bitterness to take root inside of us. Instead of living bitter, let's live better. This happens best when you are living in close relationship with others. Just like this verse above says, "look after each other." Do you have anyone close enough to help keep you from comparison, bitterness, all sorts of evil? Sometimes the problem is we don't let anyone in enough to call us out in truth and love. That's what we'll talk about tomorrow. Today, end your day with thanksgiving and gratitude. Go write "thankful" on your mirror and thank God for this beautiful life you've been given. **You are unique, an original masterpiece.**

I AM UNIQUE.

SOUL WORK:

Add a "thankful" note to your mirror.

Write down 3 things you're thankful for about your physical body.

Write down 3 things you're thankful for about your inside: strengths, character, values.

When thoughts of comparison come up, choose to celebrate instead.

SONGS:

"You & You Alone" by Upper Room Music
"Grateful" by Elevation Worship
"Thank You Jesus" by Hillsong

i'm thank-

ful for

#lookatyougirl

"For just as each of us has one body with many members, and these members do not all have the same function, so in Christ we, though many, form one body, and each member belongs to all the others."
- Romans 12:4-5 NIV

CHAPTER 5

feedback

CHAPTER FIVE

We belong to each other. Just like our bodies have many different members with different functions, they belong to each other. So it is with us, with people, the body of Christ. Feedback, huh?
I probably would have asked myself this question a while back: what about feedback? I was debating on calling this chapter either Feedback or Friendship Friday. I decided that the purpose of this chapter is to remind us, in order to see ourselves the way God does more clearly, it is extremely important to have good feedback from others in our lives. Those others are not always friends, it could also be family members, mentors, teachers, leaders, pastors, coaches or really someone who simply has insight into your life for a season and offers feedback that is helpful and sometimes life-shifting.

What is feedback? I'm not talking about the high pitched sound that comes from electrical equipment, although it may give you that same cringe-worthy feeling when we get some hard to hear feedback. We're talking about the vital communication skill that can enhance our lives tremendously. When we have healthy amounts of feedback in our lives, we truly see and know ourselves better. Feedback is essential to living a full life. We belong to each other and need to communicate when we see things that are both encouraging and discouraging. Good feedback can help keep us on the right track or steer us clear of a downward spiral. Feedback from friends and trusted people in my life has helped me take responsibility to do my creative best with my own life. It has encouraged me to walk in the right direction, and other times helped me overcome a blind spot in my life. Imagine training for the Olympics but having no one to tell you how fast you're running or how high you're jumping. You would never know if you needed to improve or if you were going the right pace. My husband had this beat up old minivan passed down for years in the family. The entire dash was electric and one day it died, so he drove across the country from Florida to California without a speedometer. Can you imagine? Driving cross country and having no clue what speed you were going? That would be extra challenging. He had to base his speed on the other cars around him, which is great that it worked out, but how much more helpful would it have been to have a working speedometer? It reminds me of the seasons when I've had healthy feedback in my life. They were way smoother and I wasn't having to work harder to know my speed, my pace. I had people helping to point out my blind spots, helping me stay in my lane, telling me I was going too fast and rushing by life and people, or that I was going too slow and needed to stop making excuses.

Feedback is so formative to our personal growth. I've had friends call out both the gold and the dirt in me, that has led to phenomenal levels of growth. I can see myself clearer when I have people close enough to be able to help me see my blind spots. In order to have healthy feedback in your life, you have to let people in close enough and welcome it - invite it really. I know that can be easier said than done, but I promise you it is worth the work and the investment in close relationships. It is not good for us to be alone. Again, we can take this all the way back to the beginning in the garden, when God said, "it is not good for the man to be alone." The enemy would love nothing more than for us to be completely isolated, or at least believe we are. When he gets us alone, he can get us stuck in a corner believing so many of his stupid lies. So often when we're in the middle of our mess, the lie creeps in that "you're the only one," "if they only knew," "no would can ever know," or "no one would understand." All of these thoughts make us feel shame and are meant to keep us silent. Sometimes these are with huge issues in our lives or even just the small daily quirks about us. C.S. Lewis said, "Friendship is born at the moment one says to another, 'What? You too?! I thought I was the only one.'" Isn't that so true? I always joke and like to change up the word and steal his quote... C.R. Zick says, "Freedom is born at the moment one says to another, "What? You too? I thought I was the only one?!" When we see someone that has blazed a trail and come out on the other side, when we see their victory, we taste the freedom they have and know that it's possible for us. That is what happens when we share life with one another -- friendship and freedom. Community is so important. Relationships make us rich. We were designed to have companionship, relationship and friendship.

"Agree with each other, love each other, be deep-spirited friends. Don't push your way to the front, don't sweet talk your way to the top. Put yourself aside, and help others get ahead. Don't be obsessed with getting your own advantage. Forget yourselves long enough to

lend a helping hand."
- Philippians 2:1-4 MSG

Do you have deep-spirited friends? Have you ever felt like you were in a crowd of people, maybe even a small community, yet you still felt all alone? Or you may be known on the surface but you've always craved for more or wondered if more was possible. I have found this to be so common. We're yearning for people to be real with us, wondering what people are really thinking or even where they would rate our friendship or level of importance in their life. What's funny is we think these games would end when we're young, but that's not always the case. Sometimes we end up being in our thirties and still yearning for more, friends you can be truly known by. Relationships where you can "let your hair down" and be all of you without fear of rejection.

"Love from the center of who you are, don't fake it.... Be good friends who love deeply, practice playing second fiddle. .... Get along with each other; don't be stuck up. Make friends with nobodies; don't be the great somebody."
- Romans 12 MSG

Don't fake it. You need a space in your life where you can be truly known and truly loved. We need feedback from others who know us deeply, who can tell when we may be "faking it" and need to be called out. The goal is to surround yourself with friends who tell you what you need to hear, not what you want to hear. I can't tell you how many late nights I've walked away from my core group feeling more known, seen, understood, and loved because of the feedback from friends. They see our blind spots; they hear the lies in between the lines of the stories and scenarios we're sharing. They can help us see the big picture, or the fact that we may just be plain wrong and need some good 'ol loving correction.

I'm not going to say it's not hard, or that things won't ever get messy, that there won't be trying moments— but I can tell you for sure: IT IS WORTH IT. It's time we stop complaining about the lack of closeness and friendship in our lives and do what it takes to create community. You could be the one someone else is waiting for. Our insecurities and fears can still scream at us, whether we're fourteen or forty-four, lying to us about what others think about us or that "you're the only one". I used to wonder if any one else desired what I was looking for. Could I be the only one who wasn't satisfied with surface-level chatter? I wanted more. Guess what sister?! There is more, I promise.

Maybe you're like me: you've had good friends for years and you're really close, but you kept wondering if there could be more? Show your gratitude for their place in your life. Continue to invest in your friendships and in helping each other grow. Affirm their role in your life and celebrate what you have. Can there be a little more depth to your conversations and friendship? I'd say yes. There is more; it simply takes intentionality. You won't arrive there on accident. Be intentional about who you spend your time with and how. Your time is so valuable and relationships are so important, make the most of the moments.

"Avoid godless chatter, because those who indulge in it will become more and more

ungodly."
- 2 Timothy 2:16 NIV

I remember the first time I read this verse underlining it in my Bible. I loved it and it's always meant a lot to me. I wanted to have friendships with purpose. I believed in more, in making meaningful connections. I'm not suggesting every hangout is a Bible study and you have to pray every time you're together. In all honesty, none of my friendships look like that. It means having conversations about what matters most and what's going on inside. When you talk about the in depth things of the soul, it won't stay surface level. Then it might turn into a friend praying for you, speaking words of promise and truth over you, and declaring God's goodness in your life.

 If this is something you are craving, then you're going to have to put your brave pants on and go for it. I went to what I call a "blind coffee date" with someone I'd heard of and connected with on Instagram. (One of the reasons I do love that square world.) We had an amazing coffee and connect one morning and during that convo she invited me to join her at an event in Dallas. I said yes. Crazy right, I realized I was flying to a city I'd never been to, sharing a hotel room with a woman I'd met for a little over an hour and going to this huge red carpet gala surrounded by zero people I knew. I loved it and I learned so much from that experience. Not to mention that friendship has grown. While there, she had a brunch setup with someone she knew locally and invited me, so with more bravery, I said yes. (This is also just creating a habit of loving yourself and being confident regardless of the outcome and nonsense expectations) That meal, shared with those two women, was so amazing. Both new friends, brand new conversations with little to no history shared and she asked, "what lie have you been believing in this season?" So rather than just connecting on surface-level content, which would've been easily done— we went for it. Did I have to fight off lies that came into my mind like, "you have nothing to offer", "they don't care what you have to say", "you are a fraud" - sure. As I've gotten older and continue to go after this, I've learned how to quickly turn down those lies and dismiss them completely. To turn up the truth, of "what I have to say does matter", "what I carry is powerful," "my stories of my journey with God will strengthen them", "you are a hope dealer". I share that story to encourage you that I'm not sure the lies will ever be completely gone, the assaults on our identity and character, but your power to dismiss them can grow stronger. It's like working out a muscle. My identity muscle is becoming stronger and stronger with every lie I dismiss and every time I choose truth. You see, one question made the difference. It opened up the deep soul talk I'm always yearning for. It would've been so easy for them to "catch up" and make small talk with me about who I am and what I am up to. We're all in the ministry world and could've chatted about that for hours. Instead we shared tears and powerful moments together. It is crazy how being intentional with one question can be a major game changer.

This may feel awkward at first. I fully understand that. One of the first intentional decisions I made was to start "The Breakfast Club". Years ago, I found myself surrounded by many friends, women I loved, but our busyness and raising babies kept us distracted and often surface-level. It would be hard to have meaningful conversations with toddlers pooping in the kiddie pool and throwing tantrums. So I simply made a little Facebook group and calendar event and picked one Saturday a month that we would leave our babies with our husbands and gather for brunch. It worked! It was also awkward at times. Conversations about our children and motherhood all came easily, and are great! Sharing seasons together is powerful. Then whenever I changed the topic and went for it, asking a deeper soul question it was almost laughable. It became the running joke like, "Here comes Cait with her heart questions." We decided to sometimes just share our "highs and lows" from the month. That is a simple and smart way to give room for heart talk. People can decide on their own how in-depth they want to go.

Let's dive into how to find friendship without forcing it or faking it, because we are in a time when true, deep friendship is flailing. Especially for our younger generation, it seems we've traded face-to-face friendship for that via a screen. I think I'm in a good spot to speak to both sides; I'm old enough to have grown up before the iPhone, social media and texting were a thing. I'm also young enough that I am social media savvy, prefer texting over a phone call, and was in youth ministry for thirteen years. When I was younger there wasn't even call waiting yet. I remember I felt like a princess when my parents got me "my own line" for my bedroom. I had my own phone number, caller ID and answering machine. I would talk on that little corded phone in my room for hours to friends and my boyfriend. Conversation now is often reduced to 152 characters or abbreviations and emojis. Relationships don't have near as much communication as they used to. Sometimes forming friendships feels like a high-risk dating experience where you're not sure what to do next. Do I call? Do I text? Do they like me more than I like them? Are we friends "like this" or "like that"? TBH, to be honest, I'd have to say this isn't something that ends in high school or college. My friends in their thirties are still having the same thoughts and concerns in finding friendship.

Look, I know this can be a very very sensitive subject. You may have been hurt, betrayed, lost trust, or simply feel unwanted or unloved. I'd love to spend a whole chapter on just that. If that is you, forgiveness is key. Forgive, get healed from the inside out and be brave to step out again.

"Make a clean break with all cutting, backbiting, profane talk. Be gentle with one another, sensitive. Forgive one another as quickly and thoroughly as God in Christ forgave you."
- Ephesians 4:31-32 MSG

Maybe you've put yourself out there time and time again and you are feeling major rejection. First of all, I am so sorry. I wish I could show you empathy over good lattes and get you a cookie. BUT don't give up. Keep being brave. I will say, make sure the people you're putting the asks out too aren't only people that you perceive to see in the spotlight of your community. Sometimes we gravitate to those whose lives are at max capacity already and wonder why they can't do coffee. When there is more than likely someone in your similar season of life who is feeling the same way you are. It takes being brave, making the plans and sending an invite. Betrayal, here is something I haven't personally had to walk through and for that I am thankful. If you have, I'm so sorry, sister. Don't allow one person's actions and poor choices to build up walls like a fortress around your heart. I promise you, it's worth it. If you've never been in a healthy, uplifting friendship, find someone who has and ask them for tips or to simply pray for you to find that friendship. If we were having coffee and chatting I'd tell you something like this:

Having friendships with strong women who are committed to me has been transformational. It's made me a better follower of Christ, daughter, friend, sister-in-law, wife, mother and leader. I can point to the largest moments of change in my life and name a friend who walked me through it, prayed for me, gave me godly advice, supported me, and encouraged me. Or brought me coffee, that was just the cherry on top. Also, friends who've simply had my back so I knew I wasn't alone when going through the hardest times. Hard moments like miscarriages, a loved one in rehab, counseling through my trauma, transition to a new season, the list goes on. Friends make the hard times so much more doable and they make the good times shine. Celebrating big moments in our lives is always better together.

"Carry each other's burdens, and in this way you will fulfill the law of Christ."
- Galatians 6:2 NIV

So what are you waiting for? Stop waiting and start creating. Create conversations that matter. Turn your "I wish" thoughts, into "I will" plans. It may not be convenient or comfortable, but it may just be what leads to your breakthrough. We belong to each other. We can dismantle the insecurities in each others' lives. On the other side of your invitation is someone waiting and wanting it just like you. Find your tribe, your girl gang, your core group. Whatever you want to call it, find it or define it with more depth and intentionality. This is one of my core beliefs around friendships: different reasons for different seasons. There will be friends who are merely in your life for one special reason or for just a short season. PSA: THAT IS OKAY. Not all friendships will look the same over your lifetime. There are seasonal friends and lifelong friends. That sounds hurtful to say maybe, but I have found it to be true. Especially if you live a transient lifestyle, for example: military life, college years, missionary, and more. I am not saying you only love them for a season but your intimacy is greater during that time. You may stay connected, but not on the same level and that is okay. Proximity creates intimacy. It's those that are nearby, doing everyday life with you that you find yourself close to. This isn't necessarily the rule, but it is common. You may have a friend you can keep in touch with long distance, but it's vital to find those in your surroundings to "do life" together. Friends help you grow into who God made you to be.

Now, I'm going to make this really practical for a bit. I don't want you to just be inspired, I want you to be ready to go. Regardless of what season you're in, you can make it happen. Think about how ridiculous it is for us to say we're "too busy" for relationships. Busy is not a badge of honor. Your schedule doesn't make you significant. You can ask God to increase your capacity for this; ask Him to show you creative ways to make this work in your calendar. This might be messy if you're in the thick of motherhood. Plan the messy play date where you show up at a park and forget diapers & your toddler's shoes. Or invite them to your house and go ahead and leave the sink full of dishes and Cheerios on the floor. Wear the shirt with spit up and the same yoga pants from the last two days. Showing up is better than trying to dress it all up. You know when you're shopping and something has an "AS IS" sticker on it, maybe there is a missing button or a snag. Your attempt to connect doesn't have to be perfect for it to work. You don't have to get fancy or pretend to be someone you are not to find a friend. "AS IS"- those are the kind of friends I want. Maybe you live a busy life in the office — we have a million excuses for why we can't leave our desk for lunch and I'd say most of them are unhealthy. We will be better worker bees when we step away and get some air (& food, always food) and share life with someone. Maybe it's 30 minutes, maybe you have the 1.5 hours. Whatever you can make work, it'll be worth it. So here's some practical tips:

Be brave. It may feel scary, it may feel hard, you may have been hurt in the past. Keep moving forward. Be brave and decide you are worth it.

Schedule it. Look at your calendar and find time once or twice a week that you could schedule in meaningful connection. It could be a quick coffee date, a lunch, dinner, overnight. The more full your schedule, the harder you will have to fight to make this happen. I'll say it again: it is worth it.

Be intentional & vulnerable. Stay intentional and committed to pursuing time for deep relationships, not only with a friend but maybe a mentor or someone you are going to mentor. Your level of transparency and vulnerability will determine theirs.

Consider a core group. Maybe you already are in a community or church where small groups exist, but you have been hesitant. Step out, try it. If not, create one.

A great starting point for a new group or increasing intentionality in your current group: **simply share highs and lows of the last few weeks**. This is a great way to start, people can decide how in depth they want to share.

Rotate who plans the topic of conversation or chapter from Scripture and they can prepare two questions for everyone to answer.

Do a book club together once or twice a year to ensure growth in your time together.

Instill intentional plans on how often you're going to gather and make sure you're all on the same page of commitment levels.

Identify who is in your inner circle that you could give an "all access pass" to. This might be 1-5 people that you would want to give "permission" to call you on just about anything and everything, those who help you see your blind spots.

A Note on Finding Your People: When you're starting to really connect and do life together, it's important to DTR- define the relationship. Honestly, in adulthood I've had so many conversations with friends I've considered sisters that were so challenging and so good. Moments where we were communicating what we'd made assumptions about or read into. Times one of us was pulling away out of fear of rejection or loss, or reading into something said or not said. These conversations never feel convenient but they always end up with so much clarity. I one hundred percent would say these times would be best shared face-to-face, but the procrastination of that happening in reality sometimes just drives the wedge further and further while you wait for that "perfect moment" to happen. Send a text and say, "I may be totally off but I felt this way when you... Can we chat later?" I've ended up having these conversations over text, Voxer, Marco Polo because of being in different time zones and schedules not lining up to even talk in real time. It always feels better. We all have blind spots in our lives, things we don't see about ourselves that we would hope the people closest to us would help us to see and save us from crashing. Most of the time because of lack of depth or lack of feeling like they have "permission" to speak into our lives in that way, they say nothing. I remember realizing the only person in my life with was willing to give me feedback was my husband. Although that is right and healthy, I needed some girl friends in my life with this access too. So I've joked with my friends for years about actually giving them a tangible "ALL ACCESS PASS" into my life. Think about what that kind of badge communicates. It is an honor to wear that in some environments. It shows mutual trust. It gives permission to go places other people cannot. You get to see behind-the-scenes, not just the highlight reel. This gives them permission to speak the things you need to hear even though it may be uncomfortable. Who would it be in your life that you'd give this to, that you'd say I need to hear your feedback and you have "permission" to do so. Tell them how highly you value their voice in your life. These could be friends or mentors, family even. Here's a cute little illustrated All Access Pass. Take a picture of it and text it to the people in your life who you would like to give this to.

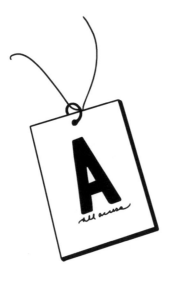

My current core group is amazing and I can brag on what has been established here because I'm a total newbie. I've been with them at this point for just over a year and they've been meeting for over five years. When they invited me to join, they made the commitment level clear. We're all moms and we meet every other Wednesday night, rain or shine, get a babysitter if you have to. It's really not difficult, it just sets a precedent of prioritizing growing relationship. At our Christmas party, our husbands joined us and shared some sweet highlights from the past year and hopes for the next. My husband said something that profoundly impacted me. He talked about how amazing it has been to watch me grow exponentially here in such a short amount of time and attested it to my group of five friends. Being around such strong and powerful women has brought me to another level of healthy identity. There's an old quote that says, "Show me your friends and I'll show you your future." So true. My life path is significantly impacted by those who are running beside me. Those who link arms with me, believe in me, pray for me, encourage me, correct me, call me up higher. Same for you sister. Who is running with you? **You are not alone.**

I AM NOT ALONE.

SOUL WORK:

Identify who in your circle you get feedback from.

Ask them for feedback: 1 compliment + 1 critique

Set a date with someone (new or old).

SONGS:

"Friends" by Michael W. Smith
"That's What Friends are For " by Dionne Warwick
"Lean On Me" by Bill Withers

"You're blessed when you
get your inside world—
your mind and heart—put
right. Then you can see
God in the outside world."
- Matthew 5:8 MSG

CHAPTER 6

Saturday

CHAPTER SIX

We are so much more than what we see. Think about how much of our time, our thought life, and our money we invest into what's on the outside. Constantly thinking and caring about the size and shape of our body, our skin, our hair color and style, our makeup, our clothes and shoes and purses. I'm not saying all or any of this is bad; what I am saying is it's a loss when we're not willing to spend anything on investing in our souls or even taking a look at what's going on inside. Do we even know what we mean when we say our inside? Our soul, which is made up of our mind, will and emotions. Our spirit. Our character. Our moral makeup. It's much easier to take notice of our skin, our hair, our waistline, our chest size, our clothing... the external. I want more than a beautiful body, I want a beautiful soul. I want to be a woman who has the mind of Christ; a free, yet simultaneously surrendered will; and emotions that add to her life, not deplete it.

"...not primping before a mirror or chasing the latest fashions but doing something beautiful for God and becoming beautiful doing it."
- 1 Timothy 2:10 MSG

Makeup and fashion can be fun, I am not saying they are wrong. We can have fun with it and use it to express our unique style, personalities and preferences. I am simply wanting us to take notice today how easily we invest our lives into these temporary, external things and how hard it seems to live on purpose and invest in our inner world. Think about it: we could have appointments every six weeks for our hair or every two weeks for our nails. Maybe we go every other month to get our eyebrows done. The list could go on and on-- eyelash extensions, facials, tanning beds, botox. It is amazing how long this "things to do" list can be for women and our appearances while we spend no time or money investing on our inside world. We do "all the things" and wonder why it still doesn't feel like enough. It reminds me of these old Discover card commercials.

Hair: $200
Jeans: $80
Shoes: $50
Eyebrows: $25
Makeup: $125
Nails: $40
Skincare: $180
Eyelashes: $80
Inner Beauty:

priceless

True inner beauty doesn't have as high a monetary price tag but it does cost you. It costs your time and intentional effort to be beautiful from the inside out. Remember how it says in Philippians 4:8, to fill your mind with beautiful thoughts. We can retrain our brain to line up with the word of God rather than the lies we're surrounded by. Our emotions can also come into alignment with the truth of God instead of being overwhelmed by circumstances. Our will can be strong, yet surrendered to our Heavenly Father who knows our needs before we even ask, who began a great work in us and promises to finish it (Philippians 1:6). Sometimes the financial investment that comes with having a healthy soul may be a professional counselor or therapist. Isn't it crazy how we make up excuses for why we can't afford to do that, yet we can easily see ourselves buying that new pair of shoes we've been eyeing or make sure we get our hair done? We wouldn't trade our monthly tanning or mani/pedi bill to see someone who can help us get healed from the inside out. Could it be that counseling isn't actually "too expensive", but that we just don't have a high enough value for it? It felt like a major financial sacrifice when I committed to regular counseling. We were young marrieds with one toddler and pregnant with our second child, living on one youth pastor's salary. It actually felt impossible. There was a season when we met bi-weekly because I couldn't afford to see her every week. That is okay. I refused to settle for not being healthy. I knew I needed to do this inside job. It was also very hard mentally and emotionally to want to go. I always compare it to the gym. It feels so hard to get there, but when you leave, you are so thankful that you went. I would hope my counselor would cancel almost every time. The inner work was hard, but it was so worth it. I felt so much better, clearer, and freer after every session. Are you willing to pay the price to be beautiful from the inside out? We need to place more priority on what is "unseen".

"The LORD doesn't see things the way you see them. People judge by outward appearance, but the LORD looks at the heart."
- 1 Samuel 16:7 NLT

We live in a world where it is easy to avoid the conflict that may be arising in our heart, the inner turmoil or distress we may be in. We put a bandaid on it and keep moving on. Your home, social, and cultural environments play a huge role in building your perspective of this issue. Whether you consistently "stuff" emotions and struggles until you blow up, thinking it will go away on its own, or maybe you honestly have really toxic thinking patterns that consume your life and you've never known there could be a healthy way out. Do your emotions run you and you feel out of control? There is so much hope and clear pathways for us to be mentally and emotionally healthy.

With all of this talk about having a healthy soul, being beautiful from the inside out and our inner world; I better define what I mean when I say soul. Soul is the inner life of a human being. Our soul is made up of our mind, will and emotions. You could also say your thoughts, choices and attitudes. It is what makes you, uniquely you. It is where your mental and emotional health can be checked. The Bible says we are made up of our spirit, soul and body.

"May God himself, the God of peace, sanctify you through and through. May your whole spirit, soul and body be kept blameless at the coming of our Lord Jesus Christ."
- 1 Thessalonians 5:23 NIV

It is hard to avoid when our body is sick: sneezing, coughing, runny nose, vomit and diarrhea. I know, I know, TMI (too much information.) For real though, we always have to take notice when our bodies are breaking down and either use some home remedies, get extra rest and potentially go see a professional for help. It is much, much easier to avoid or not even notice at all when our soul is sick. We have regularly scheduled physical check ups, dental check ups - I have to go to the dermatologist every six months for a check up to make sure I don't have skin cancer. Imagine how helpful it would be to schedule ourselves a soul check up. Listen, we know the enemy is deceitful and cunning. Imagine how much he must hate the idea of people looking inside and getting healthy and strong. Being mindful about what is going on inside, he would much rather get us distracted by the external things that don't really matter. Often our faces are stuck inside our phones and we don't even know what is going inside our hearts. We can tell you more about someone else's lives from their highlight reel because we are trying to hide from our own reality. He doesn't always have to defeat us, but merely distract us. When we live focused on and distracted by the temporary external things of the world and ourselves, we lose sight of what matters most. Our spirit, our soul-- who we are from the inside out. The things that are destroying us internally are often disguised as normal. We have to remember this world is not our home, we are just passing by. When we live with eternity in sight, we change the way we do things. Oftentimes, we get so stuck in what's in front of us we forget that.

"Don't shuffle along, eyes to the ground, absorbed with the things right in front of you. Look up, and be alert to what is going on around Christ— that's where the action is. See things from his perspective."
- Colossians 3:1-2 MSG

Most of my teenage years were spent obsessing about my outer appearance, I don't think I ever intentionally made decisions about by inner world before I became a Christian. I spent a lot of thought, time and money on trying to fix my skin specifically. I had terrible cystic acne. My parents were so kind to do whatever it took for me to find solutions for this. It was embarrassing, it was painful, it was for sure the most "self-conscious" part of the outside me. They spared nothing as I went to many treatments from facials with dry ice and extractions, multiple dermatologists, different prescription drugs, so many skin care lines and even expensive laser light therapy. We would typically find a temporary solution that would work for a bit, and ultimately leave me frustrated. Years later, once I was on my own in ministry school and then as a young pastor on a small salary, those trips to the dermatologist became non-existent. My skin was somewhat better, but I also just got more comfortable in my own skin. It didn't define me anymore and I learned to value who I was so much more than how I looked. Truly. So back in 2010 I went to my annual dermatologist appointment and found out I had skin cancer on my back. It was a bit scary in the moment, but almost expected. I am an Irish girl, both of my parents and all four of my grandparents had skin cancer. They all grew up with long winters and a shortage of sunny days in New York, but I grew up in the "sunshine state" of Florida. It was kind of an impending doom we knew was coming one day. It could have been avoided if I had made some hard, inconvenient choices when I was younger. I knew it was dangerous for me, but continued to go tanning and lay out in the sun because that was the cultural norm around me. It was like a sin to be pale.

When I look back on this situation in my life it is a pretty good picture of how we let toxic and unhealthy environments distract us and keep us from what is the most healthy for our unique souls. That amount of sunshine was completely okay for some of my friends who didn't have the Irish genes and propensity to skin cancer that I had. We could be living in an environment that is toxic for us, continuing to "lay out" in the sun, slathering on tanning oil with the rest of them — avoiding what the future could hold. Except these toxic environments could be reaping depression, jealous thoughts, lack of self-control, spiraling thoughts of anxiety that we've never gained power over. Our environments impact us, but we have to decide on how much they do. I could still live in Florida but decide to sit under the beach umbrella, or lather on some sunscreen rather than tanning oil while I play beach volleyball. Knowing what's better for us isn't always enough, we have to make the momentary decisions that may seem more difficult, but in the long run we would be thankful for. Almost all of us are living in an environment that sets us up for constant comparison and discontentment. Rather than falling victim to the root of jealousy and envy, we can choose to approach social media and friends getting what we want, with a grateful heart and true celebration. Some environments set us up for being soul sick in stress and anxiety under extreme amounts of pressure to perform. Some environments totally break down our will and leave us codependent and feeling incapable of making healthy choices. Another toxic environment is where there is a lack of healthy boundaries which leads to constant people-pleasing. Sometimes you have the option to leave an unhealthy environment and you should do so. If it's an unhealthy or abusive relationship that is causing you to live in self-hatred or depression, you need to find a way out. In general, we don't have to "leave the sunshine". What we need to do is be aware of how our environment may be affecting us and make wise choices to protect the health of our soul. So if your world is sunshine and that's not healthy for you, slather on some sunscreen and limit your time in the sun. We're made to be in the toxic and dark places and bring the light. We are called to be light-bearers in these dark places.

"Don't become too well-adjusted to your culture that you fit into it without even thinking. Instead, fix your attention on God. You'll be changed from the inside out."
- Romans 12:1 MSG

"Dear friends, let's make a clean break with everything that defiles or distracts us, both within and without. Let's make our entire lives fit and holy temples for the worship of God."
- 2 Corinthians 7:1 MSG

If your environment is toxic and unhealthy for you, make a clean break with it. Limit your exposure to the places and people that are leaving your soul sick. We cannot keep normalizing and accepting being soul sick, blending in with the crowd and having the same sickness. We are to be set apart, soul healthy, followers of Jesus-- our life should look different and be appealing to those who do not know Him. We want to actually be healthy from the inside out, not just try to look like it. We must be careful to not be like the "religious" people in the Bible:

"What sorrow awaits you teachers of religious law and you Pharisees. Hypocrites! For you are so careful to clean the outside of the cup and the dish, but inside you are filthy—full of greed and self-indulgence! You blind Pharisee! First wash the inside of the cup and the dish, and then the outside will become clean, too.

"What sorrow awaits you teachers of religious law and you Pharisees. Hypocrites! For you are like whitewashed tombs—beautiful on the outside but filled on the inside with dead people's bones and all sorts of impurity. Outwardly you look like righteous people, but inwardly your hearts are filled with hypocrisy and lawlessness."
- Matthew 23:25-28 MSG

Intense, I know. This is the Bible, these are Jesus' words and warnings to the religious Pharisees of the day. I don't want to sugarcoat things for us, sisters, and have us simply learn to put on a good facade. This passage shows what we as humans could be prone to do, clean the outside so everything looks good and shiny when inside we're filthy. Outwardly looking like we've got it all together when our hearts are filled with junk. Here is the thing, if you read this and think, "I've got some work to do." That is okay, that is good. There is nothing shameful about realizing your need for Jesus, for internal health. He didn't die on the cross because He thought we would be perfect; He died because He knew we wouldn't be and we needed a Savior. Let Him be your Lord and your Savior. Let Him lead you to being healthy and beautiful inside and out. God our Father loves us as we are, He just doesn't leave us in our junk. The Holy Spirit is our Comforter, Counselor, Guide into all Truth. So if and when you find your soul is sick, whether that is now or a season in the future, remember this: there is no shame in being soul sick. It is an indicator that you need help. He is our help. He is our refuge. This is a perfect reminder for what we talked about yesterday, another great reason for our need for community. You were not made to walk this alone. Find a trusted friend and/or counselor to walk with you to freedom and wholeness, mental and emotional health.

I love how this passage says to kill off everything connected with that way of death, our old life, doing whatever we feel like whenever we feel like it. That is not our way. We have the fruit of the Spirit. Then it says these five words that can ring in your ears in moments of misstep or when you're on the edge: but you know better now. Read it:

"And that means killing off everything connected with that way of death: sexual promiscuity, impurity, lust, doing whatever you feel like whenever you feel like it, and grabbing whatever attracts your fancy. That's a life shaped by things

and feelings instead of by God. It's because of this kind of thing that God is about to explode in anger. It wasn't long ago that you were doing all that stuff and not knowing any better. But you know better now, so make sure it's all gone for good: bad temper, irritability, meanness, profanity, dirty talk."
- Colossians 3:5-8 MSG

Once we know better, we need to choose better. Maybe you're internally freaking out, like what do I do with this now?! I'm going to give you a simple soul sick quiz. This is a quick way to give yourself a soul check up and see where you may need to put in some time with yourself, the Lord and trusted counsel. Remember how I said earlier, rather than another hair or makeup tutorial I need a good 'ol soul tutorial? Let's dig in. Here are some questions to check yourself before you wreck yourself:

SOUL CHECK
Grade yourself from 1-10. 1= sick and 10 =healthy.

_____ **MIND**
How is my thought life, my mental health? How have my thoughts been lately about myself? My circumstances? Other people in my life? Have I been prone to stress, anxiety, depression, pride, jealousy, impure thoughts? What could be the root of this? Have my thoughts gone unchecked? Am I practicing taking my thoughts captive and making them obedient to Christ? (2 Corinthians 10:5)

_____ **WILL**
How has my control center been? Have I been releasing things to God or manipulating things to happen in my own timing? Have I been giving

control of my life over to someone else? Blaming
them or letting them run my life. I am responsible for
my choices, I need to make better choices in these
xyz areas of my life. I do not want to be a pushover. I
do not want to be a control freak. Have I been
making wise choices?

_____EMOTIONS
Am I on an emotional roller coaster? Do my
emotions dictate my day? Am I aware of my
emotions or stuffing them? Are my emotions
completely depleted and I'm running on empty?

We go to the doctor when our body is sick. Where do
we go when our soul is sick? When our emotions are
out of whack, when our mind is spiraling, when our
will power is shot? Isn't it funny how counseling and
therapy have seemed to get this shame cloud over
them? Like something must be really wrong with
you if you need that. What about if we didn't wait til
we were really sick and couldn't function. What if
we scheduled check ups with a parent, a mentor, a
counselor, a pastor, a leader who's invested into you
becoming your best self. What if we knew and loved
ourselves well enough to know our seasons and
where we're at in the moment. I am a huge advocate
for counseling. It took me realizing how not okay I
was to get myself to find one. There are so many lies
swarming the idea around counseling. It was a night
in tears realizing that stuff from my past was
affecting my marriage and my ability to know love
and trust my husband's motives. I thought I'd dealt
with my past, but there were still strings attached. I
can tell you now on the other side of that counseling
that it was worth every single penny, every single
minute and all of the brave moments of showing up

that it took from me. My highest recommendation would be to find a Jesus-loving, Bible-believing, counselor. We asked a friend of ours for a personal recommendation which is always helpful, too. Regardless of what "grade" you got on your soul check up and whether or not you're thinking you need to dive into discovering healthy living, here is some helpful information around all three areas.

MIND

"Do not conform to the pattern of this world, but be transformed by the renewing of your mind."
- Romans 12:2 NIV

There are discoveries being made in neuroscience that are finally catching up with the timeless truths of the Bible. Sometimes people tend to think science and faith contradict, no way. Listen, there are neural pathways in our brain that are actually physically there that mark our thought patterns. Don't get lost in the big words, let me tell it to you like this. Every thought starts out small, like a small walking trail that's freshly being made. As you revisit that thought the path gets wider. Eventually it would grow to the size of a bike lane, than a sidewalk. The more and more you think this thought, it grows into a one lane road, then a two way road, eventually into a six lane highway. Our brains take the path of least resistance, they go the easiest route. Imagine a thought pattern you have that you can't seem to stop and you wonder why. Over time you've built a six-lane highway to this toxic thought. There are entire books about this topic that are truly transformational for teaching us the power of renewing our mind not only biblically but scientifically. The main thought I want you to have as a light bulb moment is this: most often all of the opinions of others, the ideas of the world, of your social media scrolls and news feeds are moving at high speeds on your six lane highway. The truth of God, the Bible, His words to you are still a small little footpath in the brush. It takes intentionality to build that pathway in your brain to know the truth and to walk in it. I'll say it again, the truth is so foreign because the lies are so familiar. We must turn up the truth in our daily lives. If you want to change your life, change your mind. I learned this from research: "Who you are is 99% in your mind-- how you think, feel, and choose uniquely and only 1% brain and body. You tell your brain what to do. Your brain tells your body what to do. You influence the way your body works and feels. You change your brain. You can't control your circumstances but you can control your reactions. Whatever you think about becomes a reality in your brain. Observe your actions. What you're thinking, feeling, choosing. Toxic thinking actually causes brain damage. When we allow guilt, stress, jealousy, negativity to reign in our brains— we're literally causing brain damage." The cause for mental wellness is vital.

WILL

"Anyone who intends to come with me has to let me lead. You're not in the driver's seat; I am. Don't run from suffering; embrace it. Follow me and I'll show you how. Self-help is no help at all. Self-sacrifice is the way, my way, to saving yourself, your true self. What good would it do to get everything you want and lose you, the real you? What could you ever trade

your soul for? Matthew 16:24-26 MSG

The will, our choices, is an interesting topic that I would need more than a short paragraph to write all about. So let's keep it simple. God gave us free will, the freedom of choice, as a gift. Some of us have been raised being told we were "strong-willed children". I would say, ideally, we all have strong wills. Strong yet surrendered is my goal. I want my choices to be made from a place of strength, not weakness. I want to make wise, godly choices daily that reflect my beliefs and values. Surrendered, meaning I am not in full control. I'm submitted to the Lordship of Jesus Christ. He is not just my Savior and Friend, but also my Lord. It is actually freeing to say, like Carrie Underwood so beautifully sings, "Jesus take the wheel." Read the above verse again if you went over it quickly. Give Jesus the driver's seat, you get to be co-pilot. Even Jesus, who was fully God and fully man, relinquished His will to His Father. From our strong, yet surrendered wills, this should be our prayer:

"'...not my will, but yours be done.'"
-Luke 22:42 NIV

EMOTIONS

"O my soul, why are you so overwrought? Why are you so disturbed? Why can't I just hope in God? Despite all my emotions, I will hope in God again. I will believe and praise the One who saves me and is my life, My Savior and my God."
- Psalm 43:5 The Voice

There's not many more things in this life that control our decisions and our life course than our feelings and emotions. We all too often allow them to dictate our moods and perspective. Feelings seem to guide us more than truth. Feelings do have a right place, emotions were designed by God. Emotions are meant to be indicators of what is going on inside of us, not dictators of our lives. Ultimately, it must be Truth that guides us, with our feelings following behind. I once learned this brilliant visual, that has always stayed with me: it's as if our lives were a train– we typically tend to have our feelings at the front as the engine, and the truth in the back as the caboose. What would happen if we switched those around? Being led by truth and telling our feelings how to line up. Feelings will follow. I think we'd see a dramatic difference in the way our daily lives were lived. We'd find ourselves walking in more freedom and joy. In this translation of the verse, I love how direct it makes David's statement:

"Why, my soul, are you downcast? Why so disturbed within me? Put your hope in God, for I will yet praise him, my Savior and my God."
- Psalm 43:5 NIV

Put your hope in God. We need more of that kind of self-talk. We need to take that confidence and that authority over our emotions and let truth dictate our day! Speak to your own soul. I don't want to be a woman who is easily moved or shaken, my God is not. Therefore, why should I be so fickle? So when the truth vs. feelings battle wages all too subtly in my life, I will take notice– and truth will win. That's it right there. The key is to take notice when feelings are ruling our lives. I have to take action to challenge them with truth... do they line up? Or am I feeling totally off. To do this we need to be prepared with the truth of who we are and Whose we are. Remember what God says about you, what He promises you in His word, let Him speak to you in the midst of the chaos and confusion of emotions. I promise, He brings peace and truth.

"...for God is not a God of confusion but of peace..."
- 1 Corinthians 14:33 NASB

Sisters, let's end this Soul Saturday with commitment to the journey of soul health and the ability to say, "it is well with my soul." Believing we can live not in a state of confusion and unrest, but in peace because we have the gift of peace inside of us. We live with the Prince of Peace. It's the name of an old beautiful hymn with such rich meaning and history. Let it also be a declaration that to our souls it truly is well. There's a beautiful sign I've been eyeing that says this statement, I'm going to put it up in my bathroom as a reminder to soul check daily. When I see the cute little sign that says "It is well with my soul", I'll put an internal question mark. Is it well today? Is there anything I need to bring to the Lord or ask a trusted friend to help me work out?

Look at you, girl-- glowing from the inside out.

You are whole.

I AM WHOLE.

⋀⋔⋔ SOUL WORK:

Do the Soul Check.

Look at your environment and decide if there are any necessary changes.

Pay attention to your most recent emotions, what are they telling you?

Talk to a trusted friend about how your inner world is doing.

♫ SONGS:

"You Know Me" by Jenn Johnson
"It is Well" by Kristene Dimarco
"Breakup Song" by Francesca Battistelli

"Are you tired? Worn out? Burned out on religion? Come to me. Get away with me and you'll recover your life. I'll show you how to take a real rest. Walk with me and work with me— watch how I do it. Learn the unforced rhythms of grace. I won't lay anything heavy or ill-fitting on you. Keep company with me and you'll learn to live freely and lightly."
- Matthew 11:28-30 MSG

CHAPTER 7

CHAPTER SEVEN

Good day, sister! I'm so excited about today to talk about living from a place of rest. I'm not a pro, but I've learned my fair share on the journey. I'm actually sitting here writing this from a cruise ship in the middle of the Caribbean watching the sun rise while my loved ones are still sleeping. I am pretty much at the epitome of a restful place and can tell you, it feels realllllll good. I know that's not grammatical, but I meant that emphasis. The ocean breeze is blowing my hair, I've got worship music blaring in my ears, it's still and quiet as most people are still sleeping, I'm sipping some coffee and feeling at rest and on purpose all at the same time. This has been a real struggle for me. I mentioned personality tests on Thursday and one has helped me give language for understanding how I have to fight for rest. According to the Enneagram, I am an "achiever". I am always counting the ways I am being productive and getting things done. I have to be achieving something for it to feel valuable to me. I actually had a "nightmare" the other night and I woke up laughing because it wasn't really scary, while simultaneously being full of some of my greatest fears. My nightmare was me disappointing someone by not showing up on time and then not being productive or efficient enough and missing opportunity. It felt like a fight against time. All that to say, I've had to really train myself that it is okay to rest. Not just okay, but a necessity. Not just a necessity, but rather a gift.

Sabbath originates from the Hebrew word "sabat", which means to stop, to cease, or to keep. God Himself created rest and set a day apart for it. He created our entire being-- body, soul and spirit to need rest. I'm not sure He could've made a larger declaration and reminder of our need for it. When He created the whole world, every living and breathing thing, the mountains, deserts, oceans, forests, glaciers, beaches, He decided to call it all good and take a day for rest. Throughout the Old Testament we see that sabbath was supposed to be a delight and joy (Isaiah 58:13-14). When you move forward in the New Testament, we see Jesus' regular practice of pulling away for solitude and silence. He would withdraw from the crowds and His closest disciples, daily activities, people's needs, demands on His time to be alone with His Father. Even though the urgent demands of people were always in His face, He found time to get alone and pray. He would stay up in the night or wake early before the sunrise. He led by great example for us to see the value of creating a rhythm of rest and getting alone with the Father. He led by example and then gave us an open invitation to live in peace:

**"Are you tired? Worn out? Burned out on religion? Come to me. Get away with me and you'll recover your life. I'll show you how to take a real rest. Walk with me and work with me—watch how I do it. Learn the unforced rhythms of grace. I won't lay anything heavy or ill-fitting on you. Keep company with me and you'll learn to live freely and lightly."
Matthew 11:28-30 MSG**

I love this invitation from Jesus. If you're not familiar

with it, I highly recommend finding it in a translation that you love and memorizing it. Meditate on these words from the Lover of your soul and let yourself breathe deeply the rest He has to give. He says He'll show us how to take a real rest. Just walk with Him. The unforced rhythms of grace, doesn't that sound amazing? He won't put anything too heavy on us. Keep company with Him and we'll learn how to live lightly. He is the Prince of Peace. The mentality to hustle cannot take precedent to rest. We can live and lead from rest.

My husband once booked a surprise vacation to Cabo San Lucas for us that was just three weeks later. I was shocked and surprised. We'd never done anything like that before. It had been a couple of years since we had a big vacation without the kids and we for sure never booked a trip without planning more in advance. He was on the edge of burn out; he knew he needed to get away. He could tell if he didn't get to unplug and catch a breath soon, he was going to see sparks and blow a breaker. (Not that you can always jump on a plane to an exotic location, sometimes it just means a trip alone to a coffee shop, or a long drive around town to your prayer spot.) I now know we had arrived at this boiling point because we hadn't taken this invitation to regular rest seriously. We'd let the demands and busyness of life win, over figuring out how to make sabbath possible. Nevertheless, he knew he needed to unplug— to stop the demands, the pulling, the performing and just be. That was our first time where we could tangibly feel the power of pause. It's not stop, it's not eject... it's just a moment of pause.

I love a good movie night at home, cuddled on my big

couch under blankets with my most beloved people.
Where the popcorn is cheap and the refills are free.
I drive my husband crazy when I want to pause the
movie just thirty minutes in to grab a snack. He is
the type to get all set up and go the long haul, but I
actually love the power of pause. Maybe because I
feel in control where in a movie theater you are
completely out of control. If you get stuck having
to pee and can't pause—you're missing out. I love
that at home I can press the pause button and take a
bathroom break or get a snack without fear of
missing out on anything in the movie. In our lives,
we have the power to pause when we need to get up
and take a break. When life is becoming
overwhelming, your schedule has seemed nonstop,
you've been surrounded by difficult people, or you
responsibilities have maxed you out— you have the
power to pause. We don't need to live with FOMO-
fear of missing out- on what we might miss while we
pause. The world will keep spinning, people will keep
breathing, your work can wait, your loved ones will
understand, it is okay to miss an event, your social
media account will still be there. Sometimes fear of
what will happen when we pause keeps us going on
the hamster wheel, not understanding we'll be better
off after a moment of pause. This may mean missing
something you feel you "have to" do or simply
"cannot be done" without you. An event you really
don't want to miss. You need to listen to your soul
and follow the examples of scripture and take a
pause break. Enter into real rest so that you can live
from there. Just like the movie, you don't have to hit
stop— to lose the place you were at. You won't have
to start over again searching for your spot. You don't
have to hit eject, to give up completely. You can
simply say— pause — I need a break, I'll be right

back. I need a quiet moment to recollect my thoughts, my feelings- my power. You have permission to pause to gain peace in your life.

Slow is good for the soul. I had this thought quite a few years ago and created a hashtag moment around it on Instagram for others and myself to serve as a reminder to slow down. It goes against the core of my achieving motivators. So I've had to "beat myself into submission" once I came to better understand the value of rest. I began to realize I found my significance in what I had achieved that day. This is dangerous. We cannot use our achievements as our barometer for significance and success. I had gotten into the subconscious habit of doing just that. We must stop the glorification of busy and the idol of exhaustion. Create space for rest. Rather than creating long to-do lists, on your day of rest if you're anything like me you might need to make it a "To Not Do" list.

We must learn our value is not found in how full our calendar is. You are in control of your calendar, not the other way around. Now hear me, I'm all about planning and scheduling ahead. So why not schedule in your soul care? Your rest. Make it an immovable calendar appointment if necessary. When you rest you are not only following the example God left us, but obeying the Bible, accepting Jesus' invitation and getting in on the blessing of being His daughter. The people in your life who need you, rely on you and simply come into contact with you will be thankful you prioritized rest. Figure out what is restful for you and make it happen. We cannot be such a big deal that we have no time to rest. If the God of the universe did it, so can you. You can rest. To be healthy and live the abundant life He promised us, it means you rest. You live and walk in peace. I don't want us to leave this week only inspired to see ourselves differently but to practically be set up to do so. So make this happen, pick a day a week that you will intentionally go slow. It doesn't have to be the same recurring day necessarily, just schedule one— write it in your planner or mark it on your phone. On top of that, I'd pick at least one of those a month to be your sabbath. To be a day when you make sure to intentionally only do those things that really refuel and recharge you. If you haven't figured that out yet, you can spend the first few in discovery which is always fun. Maybe it looks like not setting an alarm, taking a walk in nature, starting and ending your day with worship music and Bible reading, taking a nap, finding a "prayer spot" somewhere beautiful where you live and visiting it on these sabbath days, drinking coffee with a friend and finding out how you can best be praying for each other in this season. I'm all for some Netflix and nail painting—

those might very well be a great part of your day—
but I'd say you'll be deeply rested if you've invited
His Presence into your quiet day.

We are always surrounded by noise, it's challenging
to find silence in our world.

Create a silent space— to slow the pace and stop the
race. A day, an hour, a morning, an evening. A
quiet place for just you and Him. If only we had some
space for silence so we could hear His invitation to
us, any time and at all times. He's inviting us to come
to him, to let Him carry the load for us when it's too
much for us. Burn out? Yep, He can help. A place to
be, a place where you don't have to do anything. It
serves as a constant reminder that we are human
beings, not human doings. Though there is much
to do, we have the gift of rest, to simply stop and be
still.

**"Be still and know that I am God."
- Psalm 46:10 NIV**

When we start to live in these rhythms of grace-- we
can discover a level of peace, contentment and
satisfaction that cannot be disrupted by mere
circumstances. A lifestyle we are content in all
circumstances, as Paul wrote about in his letter to
the Philippians:

**"I've learned by now to be quite content
whatever my circumstances. I'm just as
happy with little as with much, with much
as with little. I've found the recipe for being
happy whether full or hungry, hands full or
hands empty. Whatever I have, wherever I am,**

I can make it through anything in the One who makes me who I am."
- Philippians 4:11-13 MSG

The goal is to be content in circumstances not because of circumstances. That is a life of peace, not just content when everything is just as I want it to be. Living at peace whether things are perfect or not. If we could earn our own contentment we wouldn't need Him.

"You're blessed when you're content with just who you are—no more, no less. That's the moment you find yourselves proud owners of everything that can't be bought."
- Matthew 5:5 MSG

This contentment and peace is something that could and should invade all areas of our life. It's a peace unlike anything you can find on this earth. This is heaven on earth when you can know your peace, amidst any situation. We must not allow circumstances to steal our peace. Peace is a gift from Heaven. It's a gift the world cannot give. It is a reassurance that though troubles will come, we do not have to live troubled or afraid.

"I am leaving you with a gift--peace of mind and heart. And the peace I give is a gift the world cannot give. So don't be troubled or afraid."
- John 14:27 NLT

I experienced this supernatural gift of peace in one of the potentially darkest moments of my life. When

I was eight months pregnant with our fourth child, our only daughter, I was woken up in the middle of the night at 2:29am. Waking up in the middle of the night when pregnant isn't uncommon because you often are uncomfortable and adjusting and have to pee, but this was very different. I was woken up with a knowing that something horrific was about to happen that day and to trust and pray. I debated whether or not to wake Cole up or not, but decided not to. So I did that– I prayed, I trusted... and fell back asleep in peace. I didn't know what, when or who... it was just a knowing that something to my horror was on the horizon. Morning came and with the buzz of three little boys and getting ready for school and work, my moment in the night had been forgotten, until that evening, when Cole was pulling out of the driveway and accidentally ran over our youngest son. Cade was only eighteen months old. When I heard the scream and ran outside, I saw what I hope to remain as the worst sight of my life. I saw my little boy laying face down under the back right tire. The car was stopped on top of his little body. His cries became fainter, I started to yell, "Pull forward, pull forward, pull forward!" The next five minutes are the biggest blur. I scooped my little boy off of the driveway, he caved into my body, saying "mama, mama, mama." We jumped into the car and started to drive to the hospital. Through my cries and tears I said, "I knew this was coming. God told me something horrific was coming... but it's going to be okay." I felt this supernatural gift of peace deposited in me from my moment with the Lord in the middle of the night. It was a familiar, deep knowing that I'd experienced before with the Lord. My deepest thoughts were actually that he didn't even need the hospital. Obviously my husband, who knew nothing about my prayer and peace, was having a completely different experience in this state of emergency. What is a much longer story made short (you can read the full story on my blog) is that I experienced so much supernatural peace there aren't enough words to describe it. I remained calm through the trauma of ambulance rides, IV's being put in, body scans and X-Rays, tears and all. I was able to be a pillar of peace for my little boy, my husband, and the baby inside. There are so many reasons God could have given me that gift that day; I believe it was to keep my body in peace to not go into preterm labor with our daughter. The miracle we experienced that day will forever mark us. My son had treadmarks down the back of his white shirt, yet when they cut it off in the ambulance there wasn't a single mark on his body. His skin was untouched!! There was not a mark, no abrasion, not even redness. A miracle before my eyes. Our obvious concerns were then internal bleeding, bones, his pelvis, and more. After a CT scan, X Rays, blood and urine tests– everything was 100% healthy! He had a little brush burn on his left foot and that is it. Unbelievable, miraculous, thank you Jesus! As we sat in the hospital, and the "what ifs" started to flood my mind, I had this resounding knowing inside of me that said, "there is no room for fear in your family." I continued to read Psalm 91 over him and highly encourage you to read that chapter as a declaration over you and your loved ones. It says, "fear nothing" and that is what we will continue to do. We live with the peace that passes all understanding.

Fear is contagious. I was reluctant to share Cade's story at times because I knew the enemy could distort this incredible miracle into a tool to strike fear and anxiety in the hearts of mothers and people who heard it. I know what happens when we hear or see a tragedy of this kind. Normally fear, paranoia, images of this happening to our child, and all of the "what ifs" run rampant. My brother-in-law, John, heard this from God as he prayed that night: "this is My miracle, it will not become a foothold of fear for the enemy." I know firsthand when I hear or see something that could incite fear in my heart and mind, I need to be on guard, I will not give the enemy room for fear to take root. I need to renounce the spirit of fear and declare the truth.

"For God has not given us a spirit of fear and timidity, but of power, love, and self-discipline."
- 2 Timothy 1:7 NLT

So I deny fear and anxiety from stealing my time, attention or affection. If I know that fear is not from God, then I know who it is from. I kick fear out and I continually accept the power, the love and the self-discipline my Father does give. I believe faith and hope are contagious, too. Let us continue to spread those and disavow fear from having a hold in our hearts. While we're at it, let's also break up with stress. I know today is about Sabbath rest, but I believe with rest comes peace, and from there, freedom from everything that attempts to steal our peace.

Once while I was preaching at a women's retreat, I was shocked by the response of the room when they shared a picture meme about being stressed. It was like every woman there was raising their hand, jumping up out of their seat and screaming for help. It was like a massive time of confession where most of these women were owning the stress they lived under. It felt as if it would be impossible to be a woman and not be stressed. When I think back to being a youth pastor and asking the students how they were doing, the amount of times I'd hear "busy and stressed out" was heartbreaking. I believe there must be another way. Stress does not get to be the banner over our lives. I get it, in my life I feel the stress often, but I don't welcome it. When I feel the stress start to rise, rather than owning it, I tell myself it's time to go slow. Take a deep breath, from my stomach. Think slowly, give thanks. I might try to find something I can cut out from my day. I choose to fill my mind with beautiful thoughts rather than stressful and anxious ones. Read this passage twice slowly, underline or circle what stands out to you:

"Do not be anxious about anything, but in every situation, by prayer and petition, with thanksgiving, present your requests to God. And the peace of God, which transcends all understanding, will guard your hearts and your minds in Christ Jesus.
Finally, brothers and sisters, whatever is true, whatever is noble, whatever is right, whatever is pure, whatever is lovely, whatever is admirable—if anything is excellent or praiseworthy—think about such things. Whatever you have learned or received or heard from me, or seen in me—put it into practice. And the God of peace will be with you."
- Philippians 4:6-9 NIV

We live in a time of quick fixes, which has led to pills

being prescribed for everything. Now listen, I am not saying there is never a need for medicine to help us. I have loved ones who have found medicine to help enormously. What I am saying is that sometimes the solution is not a quick fix with a pill. It's looking inside and figuring out the root of the issue. We need to be taught healthy living-- body, soul and spirit. Possibly some counseling, some brain detox from negative thought patterns or beliefs, changing some poor habits, taking some things off of your plate in the current season of life. There are probably some really wise options before a doctor would simply prescribe a pill, that has other unhealthy side effects. I want the peace that surpasses all understanding that He promises. I want to train my brain and tell my soul what to think on, what to put my hope in. I refuse to let fear, worry, anxiety and stress be the narrative of my life. I will take hold of faith, peace and rest instead. Read this translation below, it's wonderful what happens when Christ displaces worry at the center of your life!

"Don't fret or worry. Instead of worrying, pray. Let petitions and praises shape your worries into prayers, letting God know your concerns. Before you know it, a sense of God's wholeness, everything coming together for good, will come and settle you down. It's wonderful what happens when Christ displaces worry at the center of your life."
- Philippians 4:6-7 MSG

In the book of Ephesians we are taught to put on the full armor of God, among all of the different offensive and defensive tools in the armor are the shoes of peace. "For shoes, put on the peace that comes from the Good News so that you will be fully prepared." Ephesians 6:15

I believe these shoes of peace serve on both offensive and defensive sides. In those days, soldiers shoes had nails in them almost like cleats to make sure they could stand firm. So you can be sure to stand on the foundation of the gospel of peace, gospel simply means Good News. We stand firm in our peace and we walk forward with it. We are peace-carriers. We bring peace into every environment we walk in. We are ready to share the Good News of this peace everywhere we go. When we look at our world, on a small or large scale, I think we can all agree it definitely needs the heavenly peace that surpasses understanding. Let's walk in this peace and show our world what a life with Jesus-- living in rest and peace-- looks like. You are a peace carrier.

If you're like me and like to create acronyms to remember things, this is for you:

R- RECHARGE your battery. "We take better care of our iPhones, we know when it needs to be plugged in and charged." What charges your body, soul and spirit? Take a break from work, from pressure, from performing and allow yourself to recharge.

E- EAT WELL. We feel better when we eat well. Yes, go ahead and get yourself your favorite treat, sure. Oftentimes in the "RUSH" of life we don't eat well. We're grabbing food quick, but choose to eat well today. Make yourself a slow breakfast or have your favorite lunch with a friend. Take time to try a new recipe for dinner. Eat well today.

S- SILENCE Spend some time in silence on your sabbath days. Quiet the noise of others opinions, social media, tv, music— spend some moments today in the silent space. Let your mind wander or maybe meditate on a scripture verse. Create space for silence. Invite heaven to speak to you.

T- TRUST Trust today that you can just be. You can trust over striving. Trusting in Him rather than striving for Him. Oftentimes, it's a lack of trust that keeps us from slowing down. It's like a giant trust fall. Kick fear in the face. Rely on Him. Believe Him at His word. Trust that rest is good, slow is good. The world can wait til tomorrow.

SOUL WORK:

Schedule your Sabbath. Find time in your calendar to regularly rest.

Increase Peace. If there are peace stealers, identify and cut them out.

Find some quiet time to be alone and listen to "Come to Me" by Bethel Music. Ask the Lord to speak to you through this song.

SONGS:

"Come to Me" by Bethel Music
"Peace" by Hillsong Young + Free
"Peace Be Still" by Lauren Daigle
"My Hallelujah" by Bryan & Katie Torwalt

I AM A
PEACE CARRIER.

I am worth it.
I am forgiven
& free.

I am powerful.

I am unique.

I am not alone.

"School's out; quit studying the subject and start living it!
And let your living spill into thanksgiving."
- Colossians 2:7 MSG

CHAPTER 8

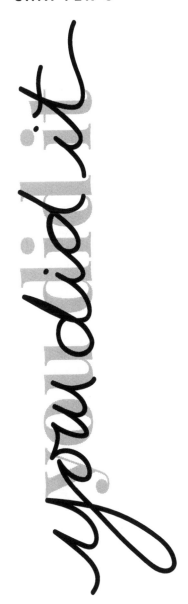

you did it

CHAPTER EIGHT

You did it; you read a book! Now you know the achiever in me just wanted to set you up for success and write a book that felt doable. You're welcome. I hope this is just the beginning. I hope you take some thoughts, ideas and principles from this little book and add them to your daily life. Take them and make them your own. In a world of so many voices blaring at us, let's choose to turn His voice up. It takes intentionality and on-purpose choices. It's not as easy as turning on Netflix, scrolling social media or picking up a magazine— but it will always feed your body, soul, and spirit truth and you'll actually feel so much better. Start your day in the Word of truth, whether that be opening Bible by your bedside, setting your daily notification for a "Word of the Day" from the Bible app or playing it on audio while you get ready by the mirror each morning. Fill your mind with kingdom reality.

"Set your minds on things above, not on earthly things. "
- Colossians 3:2 NIV

Close your eyes, look inside. Look at you, girl, from the inside out. Do you see something you love? Do you see that you are a child of God? Take a look in the mirror today, smile and what do you see? I hope this short book has served as a kickstart to you seeing yourself the way God does.

Here's a little nugget of truth for each day:

Motivation Monday
Continue to explore who you are with this new set of lenses and take responsibility for doing the creative best you can with your own life.

Transformation Tuesday
Own your whole story and let it bring God glory. Every bit of your story is forgiven and you are free from every weight that tries to hinder.

Word Wednesday
Kick out the lies that don't belong in your beautiful mind and replace them with words of truth. Let truth be your language.

Thankful Thursday
Leave thankful love notes on your mirrors and even mirrors in public places. Spread the love of gratitude over discontentment and comparison. Love the skin you're in. :)

Feedback Friday
Find your friends and welcome honest feedback.

Who has the all access pass to your life? Let them know how much you value them.

Soul Saturday
Schedule soul check ups. Invest in soul care. Look inside and see you are beautiful from the inside out.

Sabbath Sunday
You have new shoes to walk in, shoes of peace. You bring peace into every space you enter. Slow is good for the soul.

"Bye for now," that is what my Dad says every time he hangs up the phone. It's not goodbye for good; it's see you later. Bye for now. I'd love to stay connected and serve you in the future. Check out turnuptruth. com to find more truth as we're discovering it and to find a community of online like-minded women. Use the hashtag #lookatyougirl and share your experience there. I can only imagine what will happen when the daughters of the King begin to see themselves like He does.

SO YOU CAN SEE.

Identity scriptures to help you see yourself the way He does.

You are loved.
(Romans 1:7; Ephesians 2:4; Colossians 3:12;
1 Thessalonians 1:4)
> I am greatly loved by God.

You are forgiven. (Ephesians 1:7; Colossians 1:13)
> I am forgiven of all my sins and washed
> in the blood.

> I am delivered from the power of darkness
> and translated into God's kingdom.

You are powerful. (Mark 16:17-18; Luke 10:17-19;
1 Corinthians 6:19; Galatians 2:20)
> I have received the power of the Holy Spirit
> to lay hands on the sick and see them recover,
> to cast out demons, to speak with new
> tongues.

> I have power over all the power of the enemy,
> and nothing shall by any means harm me

> I have the Greater One living in me; greater is
> He Who is in me than he who is in the world.

> I am the temple of the Holy Spirit; I am not
> my own.

It is not I who live, but Christ lives in me.

You are free. (Romans 8:2)
I am free from the law of sin and death.

You are not your past. (Colossians 3:9-10;
2 Corinthians 5:17)
I have put off the old man and have put on the new man, which is renewed in the knowledge after the image of Him Who created me.

I am a new creature in Christ.

You are enough. (Colossians 2:10)
I am complete in Him Who is the Head of all principality and power.

You are an overcomer. (Revelation 12:11; Romans 8:37; John 16:33)
I am an overcomer by the blood of the Lamb and the word of my testimony.

I am more than a conqueror through Him Who loves me.

I will face troubles in this world, but I will overcome with Him.

You are gifted. (Ephesians 4:7; 1 Corinthians 12)
But that doesn't mean you should all look and speak and act the same. Out of the generosity of Christ, each of us is given her own gift.

You are an heiress. (Romans 8:17)
I am a joint-heir with Christ.

You have a purpose. (1 Peter 2:9; Matthew 5:14; Romans 8:33; Colossians 3:12; Psalm 66:8; 2 Timothy 1:9)

> I am part of a chosen generation, a royal priesthood, a holy nation, a purchased people.
>
> I am the light of the world.
>
> I am His elect, full of mercy, kindness, humility, and longsuffering.
>
> I am called of God to be the voice of His praise.

You are capable. (Philippians 4:13)

> I can do all things through Christ Jesus.

You are unique. (Galatians 5:26)

> We will not compare ourselves with each other as if one of us were better and another worse. Each of us is an original.

You are set apart. (Ephesians 1:4; 1 Peter 1:16; Ephesians 2:10; Romans 6:11; 1 Thessalonians 5:23; 2 Corinthians 5:20)

> I am holy and without blame before Him in love.
>
> I am God's workmanship, created in Christ unto good works.
>
> I am a spirit being alive to God.
>
> I am an ambassador for Christ.

You are not anxious. (Philippians 4:7; Matthew 6:34; 1 Peter 5:6-7; Philippians 4:7)
>I have the peace of God that passes all understanding.
>
>I will not be anxious about tomorrow.
>
>I cast all my anxiety on Him, because He cares for me.
>
>He displaces worry at the center of my life.

You are not afraid. (Isaiah 54:14; 1 John 4:4; 2 Timothy 1:7; Isaiah 41:10)
>I am far from oppression and fear does not come near me.
>
>For God has not given me a spirit of fear; but of power, love, and a sound mind.
>
>I won't fear, because He is with me.

You have mental health. (1 Corinthians 2:16; Philippians 2:5; 2 Corinthians 4:4)
>I have the mind of Christ.
>
>I am a believer, and the light of the Gospel shines in my mind.

You are full of joy. (Nehemiah 8:10; Psalm 3:3)
>The joy of the Lord is my strength.
>He is the lifter of my head.

You are accepted. (1 Peter 1:23)
I am God's child for I am born again of the incorruptible seed of the Word of God, which lives

and abides forever.

You are secure. (Philippians 4:19; Colossians 2:7)
I have no lack for my God supplies all of my
need according to His riches in glory
by Christ Jesus.

I am firmly rooted, built up, established in my
faith and overflowing with gratitude.

You are not alone. (Psalm 16:8; Deuteronomy 31:8)
I know the Lord is always with me, I will not
be shaken, for He is right beside me.

He goes before me, He will never leave me or
forsake me.

You are strong. (Colossians 1:11; James 4:7)
I am strengthened with all might according to
His glorious power.

I am submitted to God, and the devil flees
from me because I resist him in the Name of
Jesus.

You are loyal. (Philippians 3:14)
I press on toward the goal to win the prize
to which God in Christ Jesus is calling us
upward.